BILL WOODROW

SCULPTURES

WADDINGTON GALLERIES   22 FEBRUARY – 18 MARCH 2006

RD *You've got a show coming up at Waddington Galleries. You have said that, periodically, you'd like to change the way you make sculpture. Have you changed the way you make sculpture for this show?*

BW Yes I have, in terms of the actual physical making of it because with a lot of the sculptures I've given all the pieces to other people to manufacture. Even though I've made an original full size maquette in the studio, the final version is made by other people. There are two new materials in the new sculpture and I'm very interested to see how they work in the clean gallery space and what I think of them when I see them out there. There are some ceramic things, and some laminated MDF (medium density fibreboard) which has very strong colours. Something that I haven't used in this way before.

RD *I was quoting from a text you wrote in the catalogue for 'The Beekeeper', where you seemed to be talking about a change of subject, rather than a change of materials.*

BW Yes, I think with The Beekeeper there was, specifically, a change of subject, because, I wanted a single theme to work from for quite a long period of time rather than just going from, in a fairly intuitive way, one work to the next, and letting one work feed and generate the ideas for the next work. With The Beekeeper, I wanted a theme that would always be there, even though one work would generate ideas for the next, but because of the theme I would know what area they were going to be in. With this new group of sculptures, I didn't set out with a theme but in a strange way, a kind of theme has appeared.

RD *Which is?*

BW Well, I'm not quite sure what I would call it, there's something to do with the skull as a formal object, as a conceptual thing and I'm trying to figure out by making the work why it fascinates me, or has done over the last six months.

RD *Classically skulls are used in vanitas paintings as momento mori, reminders of mortality, are you particularly preoccupied with your own mortality at the moment?*

BW (laughs) No I'm not and I don't think that's where it came from. I don't think it originally started in that area, but that heritage is certainly in the work.

RD *They're not just human skulls are they?*

BW No, no, they're animal skulls.

RD *Where do these animal skulls come from?*

BW Well the skulls…. I was trying to figure out how I first got involved with the skulls. I've used skulls in my work in various ways since the early eighties, not very often, but every now and again.

RD *It was often a very generic human skull.*

BW Yes, but recently I'd been looking at some deer skulls and I got very interested in the way they were put together and their form. I tried, as a starting point with my ceramic experiments, to make a deer skull, or parts of it, and that got me interested even more in how the skull went together, perhaps because the one I had wasn't complete. So I spent quite a lot of time at the Horniman Museum looking at skulls and drawing them and then came back to the studio and tried to make skulls, not always directly from the drawing but from my memory. Trying to see how my memory was in terms of the form of the skull and how it was put together. And so there are ape skulls and my own made up ape-like variations. I don't think if a bone or skull specialist saw these skulls they would say; that's a so-and-so, that's a particular ape, they'd probably say, that's a very weird looking skull, in actual fact. But they seem to fit, in your sense of a generic ape skull. So there was that, and at the same time I was trying to get to terms with clay which I hadn't used before, which was an interesting thing to do. I didn't find it a particularly easy material. I needed more patience than I had at that time I think, but I learnt to wait and that proved the most important thing, that you had to give it some time. Then I was able to make some of the things that I wanted to make.

RD *The colour bases came after?*

BW Yes, the colour bases came after. I started off by making a whole range of skulls which I really liked just on their own, but on their own they weren't sculpture, they were just ceramic skulls and I wanted to use them in some way as a component of a sculpture, so the laminated coloured pieces, which I don't see as bases in your

sense of the word, become integral components of the sculpture. They are the other components of the sculpture.

RD *How are they formed? Where do the shapes come from?*

BW In the first instance with the skulls, I thought I'd like them to have a body of some sort, not to be disconnected, not just separate. But I didn't want to make a skeleton, and I didn't want to make something representational in the same manner as the ceramic skull. So I started thinking from the opposite pole if you like, of how to represent something. And I came up with this very geometric, formalised, very simple body shape, which also could be gestural in the sense that it could have some animation to it.

RD *Does the body shape correspond to the generic form of the kind of animal, the crocodile looks a bit like a crocodile, the cat looks like a cat (though it's not a cat it's a lion or a tiger)?*

BW Yes, some carnivore. Yes, it does. That was a way of getting to the form.

RD *Is that a bit like Aborigine x-ray pictures? Inverted, since the x-ray pictures generally show the backbone and a head.*

BW I didn't see it like that, it's something to do with the ceramic skull being strangely timeless, it could be a fossil, something very old, it doesn't have a fixed moment in time. Whereas the coloured laminate does seem to have a reference to now, whether it's from your kitchen or from various different artefacts that are made with it. It seems to be the opposite. The two things, the skull and the laminate are very different representations of a possible time. I think I wanted to have that mix and to have that sort of opposition.

RD *When you say the skulls themselves weren't sculpture but adding another component makes them sculpture, is sculpture multi-componented?*

BW Not necessarily "multi-componented" in that sense, but for me at that time it wasn't enough to have the skull on its own, it didn't give me enough, it was too easy to look at. There was no thinking to be done just by looking at the skull, whereas when the two very alien materials, ceramic and coloured laminate were put together the result for me was a very bizarre combination. The coloured bodies in a strange way animated the skulls, they became alive..

RD *You had all the skulls first?*

BW Yes.

RD *So then they became a group of objects. Couldn't they have just been the whole group of skulls together as one object?*

BW No, they were just a collection of ceramic skulls at that point. Material. I would have looked at them as material at that point.

RD *Why did you start working with plastic laminates?*

BW It is a material that has interested me for a long time.

RD *And why does it interest you?*

BW Because it's so manufactured and so un-handmade in its raw state. When you get a sheet of it, it tends to say; make me into some form that is very crisp and sharp, and I haven't had a reason or an opportunity to use that aspect of it. The new work presented this opportunity and it wasn't that I spent a long time looking for that opportunity, it just arose, together with a fairly conscious decision to use colour in some form. I think that interested me a lot.

RD *You'd have to be a bit more specific, because actually there's a lot of colour in your work, there's a lot of applied colour in the work as well as coloured materials.*

BW Inherent colour in the material?

RD *Yes. So in what way is this different colour?*

BW I think in terms of the relationship between the colour and the form, with this material the colour becomes more pure in a way. It's a more interesting relationship between the colour and the form. The colour on a car bonnet or car door is as pure and as bright on a lot of occasions, but the form that it's on seems to dominate, seems to be stronger in a way than the colour. The colour almost becomes secondary. Whereas with these new things I think the form and the colour are nearly one and the same thing, or perhaps a better way of putting it is that they are equal and strangely the colour becomes stronger because of that. I haven't really thought about how it works before, I've just done it. What I've found really exciting about using this colour is how strong and powerful it is and what I've enjoyed is trying to ensure that the things that I've combined with this laminate material don't get lost, hopefully preventing the colour being so dominant that you just don't see the other stuff.

RD *Where I think it's different is that having made a decision that demanded the thing to be made, then what you get back is not alterable, i.e. I'm supposing that having been made the MDF bases are then non-manipulable, (…) it becomes a given rather than an applied colour which you can change.*

BW Well I did wonder on some occasions fairly early on whether I could apply other colour on top of it to change it or if I wanted to give it some sort of texture. I could do that, I did consider it, but chose not to do it because it then…

RD *Would make them mucky I would have thought.*

BW Well, yes, not that that wouldn't be interesting but I was still concerned about how they were in their pristine state. If I lost interest in that I might start looking at other ways of working with them.

RD *How do you choose the colour?*

BW By intuition, and I don't know what the…

RD *It's to do with fit presumably?*

BW Yes it fits, I mean if you choose one colour for one skull then it seems you can't use that colour for another one, so you have to choose another colour.

RD *I think you need to say something about where the colours come from, the colour is not an infinite choice is it?*

BW No, no, it's a manufactured range, it's a manufactured colour and there's a limited range of these plastic laminates that you can put on to other materials. So you have to choose from that. I knew that I wanted to make one very bright, quite large piece that was very strong and so there was an ultramarine blue, or near ultramarine blue body on one of them.

RD *That's the crocodile?*

BW No, that's one of the apes. The crocodile skull is on a form which is more a maroony, plum colour, and what was strange was that there was actually a laminate which had a kind of crocodile skin pattern on it, which I looked at but it just seemed that the work wasn't about that. It was too obvious, it didn't work at that

point, in the way that I was thinking with associative colour. I suppose the colour gives a mood of some sort. And as I've said, once I had used one, I didn't want to use it again on another one, so I would search for another colour.

RD *I'd like to get back to The Beekeeper. I thought when I saw the show at the South London Gallery, that you were quite psychologically exposed as 'The Beekeeper', more so than in other works of yours. It was hard to get at what was going on because there were a lot of curious currents in the work and funny obsessions. And when you wrote about it you talked more in an external way about symbiosis, the relationship of bees to the agrarian economy, etc, but for me I thought that the complex figure of the beekeeper, the honey and a funny thing with money and honey was curiously sexualized. In a sense honey is the beekeeper's fluid; and whether the beekeeper keeps or spends their fluid, seems to be an issue. Other works of yours are often issue based but very rarely closed, I mean they're not propagandistic. With The Beekeeper there was a sense of invitation to understand something else, perhaps in relation to something like a portrait. I did see that there was a self-portrait of yours which both has a beehive on your head and that you're covered in dripping gold or honey. Though this work wasn't in the show I don't think.*

BW But it does exist, yes.

RD *The new work steps back a bit from that psychological exposure, do you think? Is that a correct reading for a start?*

BW I think it probably is.

RD *You might well have been going through a period of self analysis, I don't know, but I thought you were invited to understand The Beekeeper as the/an artist's figure and that the artist was yourself and The Beekeeper was gathering, saving or spending in a variety of ways.*

BW Yes, I think that the figure of The Beekeeper didn't set out to be self referential. It was never the idea that it should be me, but I can't say that it wasn't me. But I can see that this probably happened whilst I was making the stuff. And I think that The Beekeeper was always in this situation where you couldn't win but that you weren't losing, sometimes you were losing more, sometimes you were winning, a kind of situation where the harvest which kept you alive was also the thing that you got stuck in.

RD *Getting stuck in things was quite a strong factor… and the marionette figure, being a marionette, is also something which has it's strings pulled. There were also those funny bags of fluid, glass capsules of fluid, which were kind of scrotal as well as being purse like.*

BW The amber ones?

RD *Yes.*

BW Yes, they were a currency of some sort, I think you're right there. At the same time they were very beautiful, so there is a tension there because of that.

RD *Why shouldn't they be beautiful if they were currency?*

BW There's no reason why they shouldn't be. I was just thinking maybe that there are associations with currency that are… well I suppose if you go back to the old saying 'money is the root of all evil' there are those kinds of associations, but there's no reason why evil shouldn't be beautiful either, quite often it is I guess. I'm not sure about that. Maybe western currency I haven't always considered as beautiful. Quite often another culture's currency is seen as beautiful because it's not something you actually use, it has different object status. But that's sort of an aside really.

RD *If we are talking about spending, then again, the money shot in porn-movies is the shot of ejaculate flying through the air.*

BW Right.

RD *And spending is both a means of exchange but also has a sexual reference, The Beekeeper's kind of charged up with his honey, bees are fostering and nurturing…*

BW But highly reproductive.

RD *Yes, though breeding is like rabbits rather than bees. Like I say, when you talked about it you tended to talk about it in terms of something like the bee's relationship to the agrarian economy rather than the metaphor of the bee, in terms of the kinds of meanings it might have for you personally. But what I found in the work in the show was that there was this degree of psychological complexity, to do with being stuck or unstuck and with the relationship of honey to the idea of being stuck, and to the way in which the beekeeper was often bound that I couldn't fathom out but was intrigued by. It seemed to be less about storytelling and narrative than some of your other works.*

BW Right, well I'm not sure that I've figured it either in that sense.

RD *So beekeeping might have been the ostensible subject, but actually I couldn't work out what the subject was. I found it quite disturbing, the show, but not in an un-interesting way… And I'm not going to get you to talk about it am I? (laughs)*

BW Well the reason that I'm probably not going to talk about it is that I haven't actually thought of it in those terms. I think for me making the sculpture was enough. That was why, whatever it was that was generating those kinds of images, I didn't need to go back and rationalize them and figure out what it actually meant. It was just that the making of them was sufficient, because since then I certainly haven't done that, and never felt a need to. It would probably be a very interesting conversation but it's probably a very long one, I don't even know if I would want it, to be quite honest.

RD *Let's talk about roots or string. A lot of your works have stringy things in; I see roots, string, networks etc., as both supports and binding within the work. And at least two of the large scale public works have used them, the maquette for the Seafarers Memorial had a lot of rope in it. And the one in Trafalgar Square, 'Regardless of History' is about roots in a way, in that there's these three things piled up on top of each other and then there's a point where you obviously got completely engrossed in building this lattice over it of roots and with binding it and securing it to the site. Let's try and talk about that, roots, binding.*

BW Well I think there are different levels on which you can look at that. I think there has always been a linear element to my work which relates to drawing in the three-dimensional work. For example, drawing was an important element of the early cut-out pieces.

RD *Yes, the mapping process is a very strong element in those cut-outs.*

BW And I think that interest goes all through the work, that interest in the linear form, whether it be three-dimensional or two-dimensional. When it's manifest, literally in the roots of a tree, it visually has that linear form. But in terms of the work, 'Regardless of History', there was also a very clear function that those roots had to achieve. Which, for me, was to make the plinth part of the sculpture and not just a support. Literally to pull and lock the two things together, so that the sculpture wasn't just something that was plonked on the top. The plinth became an integral part of it. Even throughout The Beekeeper series there are lots of wires.

RD *I was trying to include those kinds of structures.*

BW And in this new body of work, there is one group of sculptures that are very linear because they are made from twigs that were glued together to make forms and structures. Looking back, there aren't that many things that I've made that have one continuous surface, they tend to be broken up into pieces like those structures, it's sort of unusual for me to make a single form.

RD *When we were talking about the skulls, you said they weren't sculpture. I wonder if the coloured bases weren't substituting for the roots. The skull isn't tied to the base is it?*

BW Ah, it is.

RD *Ah, so it is.*

BW You'll see it's very finely tied with gold wire.

RD *And it wraps over the skull or through the skull?*

BW It just goes through the jaws somewhere. It just holds it on.

RD *That's a practicality or part of the work?*

BW It's both. It's both. You can't just have a practicality and it not be part of the work. It's not hidden. They could be fixed invisibly, but I chose not to.

RD *Anything can be connected to anything else and you can do it invisibly or visibly and when you do it visibly then the means of connection becomes also a part of whatever it is you're looking at, so it suggests that this is tied to that and that therefore the connection is contrived rather than natural as in head to body. My head is attached to my body but it can't be disconnected. Maybe the tie implies the possibility of disconnection rather than emphasising connection?*

BW The tying of the skulls to these coloured laminate bodies, with this very delicate gold wire, does have a practical function; it stops the skull falling off, if it gets knocked. It also has a sculptural function for me in as much as it's a third element. There's the ceramic skull, there's the body, then there's this very delicate, thin gold wire… And it was important that it was a precious material used in a way normally reserved for something quite cheap and throwaway. I wanted it to show in the same way as the process in my early cut-out works where it was always upfront and very obvious how the things were made and put together.

RD *In the cut-out work, there was the mental act of projecting the net on to an already complex, three-dimensional surface. To be able to achieve something which then folded up to form this other thing was an extraordinary act of mental projection. One of the things that always intrigued me was the thin strip of metal connecting the source object with the folded construction, an umbilical connection. I remember a rope coming from a photograph in an earlier work of yours that did the same thing. Does the gold wire have a similar connotation? It's not an umbilical link or a parental link but you're saying it is something which needs to be there.*

BW It needs to be there and although it's physically a very small and very slight part of the whole sculpture, it has for me as much value as the other much larger parts. It's a very important part of it. It's something that you could easily walk past and miss. But for me, it's important, purely because the way it works formally as a very thin linear element in contrast to the bulk of the body and the handmadeness of the skulls. I really enjoy these three very different elements.

RD *Why gold? It is something that occurs often in your work, either as gilding or as gold paint or as money or as ingot shapes.*

BW This wire is the first real gold I have used.

RD *What's it about then Bill, the gold?*

BW What interests me about the gold is that it is a currency that occurs almost universally, apart from in some aboriginal cultures which you might call leaf cultures where they don't mine things, as opposed to stone cultures where they do. And it has acquired a great universal value. I find it fascinating how an inanimate mineral can have such value and how it got chosen against other things… because it has lots of qualities other things don't have.

RD *It doesn't age.*

BW It doesn't age, it doesn't tarnish, it has great working qualities. It's difficult to get hold of so it has a market and scarcity value. It seems that people spend most of their lives trying to accumulate it in some form or another and as such I use it as a symbol of wealth. Most people work for money, which you can translate into gold in some way. Finance is a very key part of everybody's life. I think gold is just a very obvious way of talking about that and people's ideas and fantasies of achievements or non-achievements.

RD *And is there a difference between using real gold and making things gold?*

BW Yes, there has been. As you rightly picked out, this is the first time I've used real gold apart from gold leaf which is a step up from gold paint. These are all illusory things, a magician's way of making gold if you like where you end up with something that actually doesn't have value but it has a surface appearance of something that is valuable. Whereas with this new sculpture, it is easy to miss the real gold wire. Most people won't know it is gold wire unless they read the label. It is doing the reverse of making an illusionistic piece of gold. It just looks like a bit of brass wire, so the gold becomes my personal piece of knowledge.

RD *Well it would be kind of cheap if it was covered in loads of bling, it doesn't necessarily imply that if you used loads of gold it would look good (laughs).*

BW No, not at all, no that's not what I meant.

RD *Well I think there's something else. Going back to that idea of one thing being tied to another, as being a connection between two parts. That seems to have some association with the roots proliferating and kind of growing all over things. In the bound books, the binding goes round and round and round and round, you know really tied up. In sewn parts the stitching is sometimes very extensive and very definitely closing something. On the other hand the flat strip of metal that occurs in the cut-outs has this very strong umbilical connotation. All of these are very evident. If you reduce that down to a thin sliver of wire then obviously you would make the wire more valuable because then it ceases to be utilitarian. If it's just an old piece of wire then it wouldn't signify. By upping the material value you allow it to have a connotative value. I'm not sure if I agree with you about subverting it. I think by using it you use the value of the material to undermine its utility and to increase its potential for meaning within the work.*

BW Yes, I'd hoped I was saying that at the same time, when I was talking about the three different materials and wanting the wire to have equal status because of its material wealth.

RD *By making it expensive.*

BW Yes

(pause)

BW Going back to the linear structures and things, it made me think of the difference between a chamber orchestra, and a full orchestra. What I like about chamber music, is the way you can move through it whilst you can hear all the components. A sort of space in between sounds that you can move around in. With a large orchestra, where they are all playing at the same time, you can do that, but the effect is to achieve something else which is much fuller and is not so much about the individual pieces staying individual within the whole. I think with some of these new sculptures with the linear structure, it's that chamber music quality that I like about them.

RD *I think chamber music is inclusive and symphonic music is exclusive. The point about chamber music is you can be a participant and with symphonic music you are the audience and there is a composer. Obviously there's also a composer for chamber music. With symphonic music, though the experience maybe equally profound, you're less invited to put yourself in it. Chamber music has two, three, four, five component parts…yes you're right, it's the relationship between those small number of things which constitutes the interest whereas in symphonic music there's something else that happens. It's more overwhelming.*

BW Some of these twig pieces made me think of Polynesian maps or navigational aids. I'm not sure if they're three dimensional in the sense of sculpture but they are certainly made from three-dimensional material and allow the eye to move around the map in a similar way to listening to chamber music and consequently the body to move around the ocean surface.

RD *No, they're not three-dimensional.*

BW The maps are flat, but these sculptures make me think of three-dimensional versions of them.

RD *Let's ask another question, 'history' is a word you use a lot, particularly in relationship to large scale sculpture, it's a word that occurs quite often in your titles. What is history?*

BW I think history is anything that's in the past tense and that can be up to the immediate moment. It can also be anything that we use in some way to justify the present. History can be in all forms, a book, something somebody says, or something that you remember. It's a past thing that has some sort of relationship to the immediate present. I've used, I've tried to use definitions of it before, things like: 'it's the accumulation of all the knowledge in the world'. Which is a very broad, generalised sense, but it can also be specific things.

RD *Is it a 'His'-story or 'Her'-story?*

BW It's 'their' story or it's 'our' story. I don't see it as a male or female dominated thing. I hadn't genderised it.

RD *It's something that can be used. Is it something we suffer the consequences of?*

BW Yes, on a lot of occasions the knowledge of history can be in theory very beneficial, but it's also something that really gets in the way a lot of the time.

RD *Your history books are as often shut as open. 'Sitting On History' is an open book, but the history of The Beekeeper is irrevocably shut. Which refers to the question I was trying to ask about the content, since the content is, as it were, displayed but not shown.*

BW It's there but you can't get at it.

RD *Well I can get at it, in some ways, I don't know if it is correct or not. Was that sewn book in the show? Or is it a separate work, the history of beekeeping?*

BW It's called 'Timetable'.

RD *Yes, so it was in the show.*

BW I think what interested me about that was, if you have an instruction manual, it's one way of learning about something. But if you have the manual and it's bound up, your relationship with it would be obviously very frustrating, because you couldn't refer to it. I think this frustration could become something quite positive. It is often, I think, more interesting not to refer to the manual. If it were a car manual, your car might not work at the end of it, but if it were a sculpture manual the results might be very different. It seems to be something to do with rules.

RD *Is it not to do with secrets?*

BW Well, they're not secrets because if they are in a book they are available to everybody.

RD *But the book's sealed.*

BW Yes. But, in an instruction manual, there is information and you have to read the manual to get it. The other way of getting that information is just from experience. It might be a much longer way of getting the same information, but a very different way of getting it. It's the play between those two extremes that interests me. In particular with the beekeeping manual, the information in the book about the actual methods used, hasn't really changed from when people started keeping bees until now and so it seems like a fixed almost finite block of information and time, and somehow sewing up the book was a way of not letting it escape.

RD *The book is sealed and it's in French. I mean there are two levels of inaccessibility in that. Obviously it would read differently for a French audience, and the book is also arcane, it's a tooled leather volume that implies a certain antiquity. This relates to what you say about the technology being one which hasn't developed, there are only some slight changes in beekeeping technology. So we're looking at something which is doubly inaccessible, doubly denied to us. We can't open the book and we can't read the information within it, so that's a kind of sign of withdrawal or of refusal to disclose. With that in mind you look at other works in the show, as you described, trying to find out in the absence of the book of instruction, how you are supposed to do the job at hand. As viewers to the exhibition, we are trying to unpick/unpack secrets from the show and it's probably not about beekeeping.*

BW But it just started me thinking that if there was a book of information, which is closed and bound, which you know exists and contains a set of rules or a set of instructions on how to do something, if they're inaccessible, then basically you have to figure it out yourself.

RD *You also have to know that apiculture refers to bees and not to apes.*

BW Yes, you may or you may not know that, it may intrigue you enough to go and find out what that word means, or ask somebody or look it up in an unbound book or unsewn up book.

RD *Do you look at 19th century sculpture a lot? I was in Berlin and was looking at the statue of Victory on top of a long column. It's a ridiculous monument, a very tall column with a gilded, winged figure on top of it and the column has all sorts of bits sticking out of it.*

BW No, I don't know it.

RD *Or that Columbus monument with the ships sticking out that's in New York. The accumulation of things within 19th century public sculpture has some similarities to the way that objects accumulate, the way that tokens accumulate in your sculptures. Do you think of yourself as trying to recover a language which is lost, devalued, degraded, passed over or whatever?*

BW Well, it has often been used in critical writing about my work, as a way of putting it down. Calling it very 19th century. 'Man wrestling with writhing serpent' has always been seen as a very derogatory thing to say about sculpture. Actually, I don't look at it a lot, but when I do see 19th century or even earlier sculpture, I do enjoy the number of elements that can be put together and the complexity of it, especially in some ecclesiastical carving.

RD *Well, the idea of allegory is very important in 19th century public sculpture in order that attributes are read and the allegorical is a useful way of understanding the kinds of composite images that you make. Although when you talk you don't allow the allegory in that, although the language may be allegorical, the key is lost.*

BW I'm not using a standard key to get there.

RD *By juxtaposing different things together, the only way they make sense is if they become symbolical or allegorical.*

BW Yes.

RD *Because that's the only way they become readable.*

BW Well your original question was do I look at a lot of 19th century sculpture.

RD *Yes.*

BW And I think my answer is I don't go out to look at it but I know about it.

RD *Do you not go out to look at it because you don't want to, because you're not interested or because you think it's a red herring. Why not?*

BW I don't look at it because I don't feel a need to. I haven't made any decisions that I mustn't look at that work, I wouldn't approach it that way, I don't feel a great need to. Looking at it doesn't feed into my work, it doesn't give me something that I don't already have in terms of making work. I think, for me, looking at art, looking at other people's work and then relating that to my own work is actually very difficult.

RD *It's not something you do a lot is it?*

BW No, but I do look at art and I do enjoy it, but I don't understand that it's informing my work. I don't get some sort of immediate thing from it whereas I do when looking at ethnographic objects or non art objects. I don't think it is totally to do with figuring out how things are made. I think what does fascinate me much more when looking at them is how they functioned at the time of their making and how they function now.

RD *Don't you think Nelson's Column is a pretty amazing object?*

BW Nelson's Column? Yes, and I also think Victory, the one on top of Wellington Arch at Hyde Park Corner, is an amazing sculpture. I really enjoy looking at it. There are some things about that sculpture which I think are very clever and I've only recently understood what it was and it's a very simple thing. Normally in a chariot, when you're being drawn along by horses, you stand in the

chariot and your feet are on the bottom of the chariot and only the top half of your body would show. I don't know who the sculptor was but I think they've done a very clever thing. They've realized that there's a problem with only half the body showing and they really needed it to be fully visible. So in order for the allegorical figure of Victory to be fully showing, they've filled the chariot with stuff like cannons and flags, and she's standing on top of it all so that her whole figure shows and this formally creates a fantastic sculpture. Whereas if it was done naturalistically with the person standing in the chariot then it would be really inert. I look at it every time I go past and I just suddenly realized one day it's to do with that figure standing up above the chariot and the way that that's achieved representationally. You couldn't have her floating in mid-air so you've got to fill the chariot with all this other plausible stuff that she can then stand on. I really enjoyed that. Going back to things that I might see in the British Museum, or collections of ethnographic objects, I think I really like them because they were made to have a function within a society in a way that I think very few things that we make or use today in our culture do. We don't make our own furniture, we don't make our own tools or instruments generally speaking. So these objects had this other function, which seems to be lost. I really enjoy thinking about that and guess something of that goes back into my work.

RD *But is it not also the case that 19th century sculpture functioned within a context and that one might envy the confidence that gave and the ability to construct extraordinary combinations of things. We're not talking about dead soldiers, nor dead white men necessarily, we're talking about the good ones which are incredible assemblages and the notion that the domain in which they belong was a functioning one in which allegory was readable. I tend to think that was all destroyed in the First World War, that that was when a shared language was eliminated, because the statues of victory were so empty of content for those that experienced the war.*

BW Well, the war memorial kind of took over didn't it?

RD *Yes, the war memorial did take over and became a list of names rather than anything allegorical. Though the Cenotaph, I think, is also a rather wonderful piece of public sculpture as is the Menin Gate, both by Lutyens. That complex allegorical language, I think, was rendered defunct by the experience of the First World War. When you came back, even though you'd won, a Victory didn't really do it, didn't convey what it was like to be sitting with your feet in the mud surrounded by rotting corpses. Post that then it's been very difficult to construct public sculpture with the same notion of shared allegorical stance, shared symbolic languages or complex symbolic or allegorical language. The suggestion that the large scale works that you make may refer to the tradition of 19th century monumental sculpture, is used as a negative by some critics. In fact it's something that various artists that I've talked to find interesting. The critic will use it as a kind of negative, a dismissive negative, but what other people are doing is looking at the work and finding that there's something interesting because it's a hard area to annex and it's something that has been lost.*

BW Right from being a student at St Martins, and I've said this before, it was an absolute taboo area; narrative or allegory in any form. If you're told not to do something then obviously it becomes more interesting. But there must have been something in me that drew me anyway to those kind of things and then to be told no you can't do this, really stupid if you do this, that makes it doubly interesting. It's like poaching!

RD *I think you're a poacher turned gamekeeper Bill, you don't poach any more! You haven't done any poaching for about twenty years, I wouldn't have thought!*

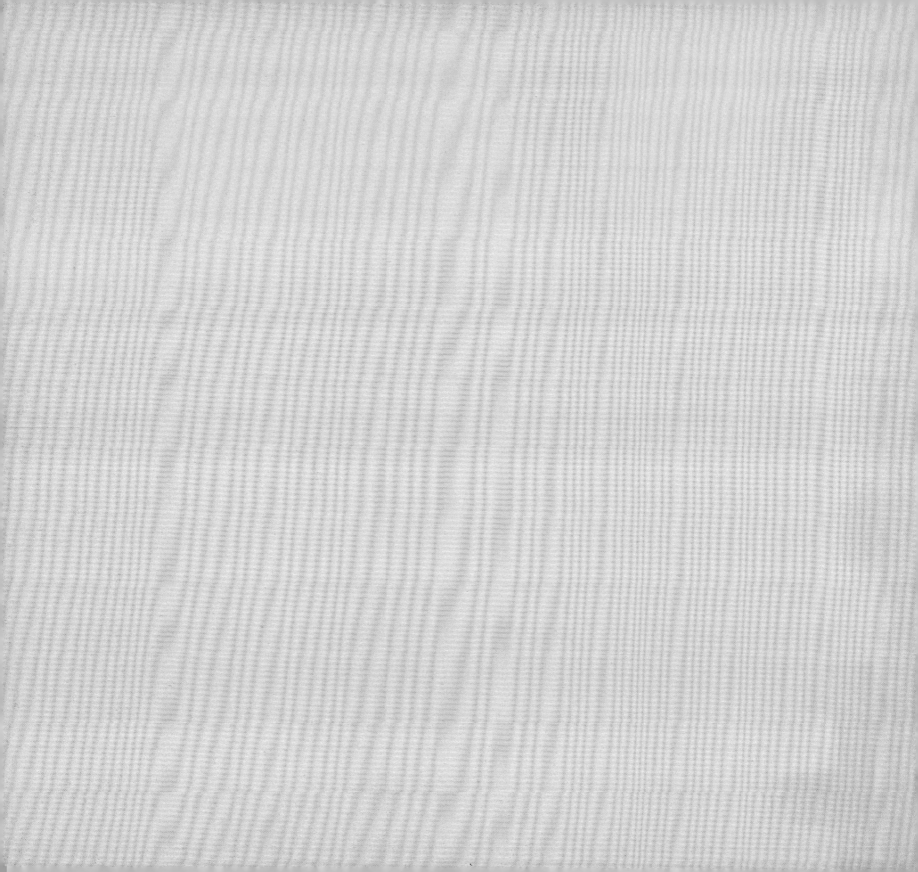

1. VERTICAL PUPA 1997

13 $\frac{1}{2}$ × 10 $\frac{1}{4}$ × 7 $\frac{1}{2}$ in / 34.5 × 26 × 19 cm
bronze, paint and wax
unique

2. **SUPPORTED PUPA** 1997

6 $\frac{1}{4}$ × 13 × 9 $\frac{1}{2}$ in / 16 × 33 × 24 cm
bronze, paint and wax
unique

3. KNOTTED PUPA 1997

3 $^7/_8$ × 9 $^1/_2$ × 13 $^3/_8$ in / 10 × 24 × 34 cm
bronze, paint and wax
unique

4. GLOBULE 1997

39 × 39 × 26 in / 99 × 99 × 66 cm
bronze, wax, gold leaf, paint, shellac and glass
unique

5. SHIP OF FOOLS WITH SMOKER 2000

41 × 24 ³/₈ × 20 ¹/₂ in / 105 × 63 × 53 cm
patinated bronze
edition of 8 plus 4 artist's casts

6. **CELLOSWARM** 2002

83 × 37 $^3/_8$ × 37 $^3/_4$ in / 211 × 95 × 96 cm
bronze, stone and gold leaf
edition of 8 plus 4 artist's casts

7. **SEPARATOR 2** 2002

67 × 42 $\frac{1}{2}$ × 34 $\frac{5}{8}$ in / 170 × 108 × 88 cm
bronze and paint
unique

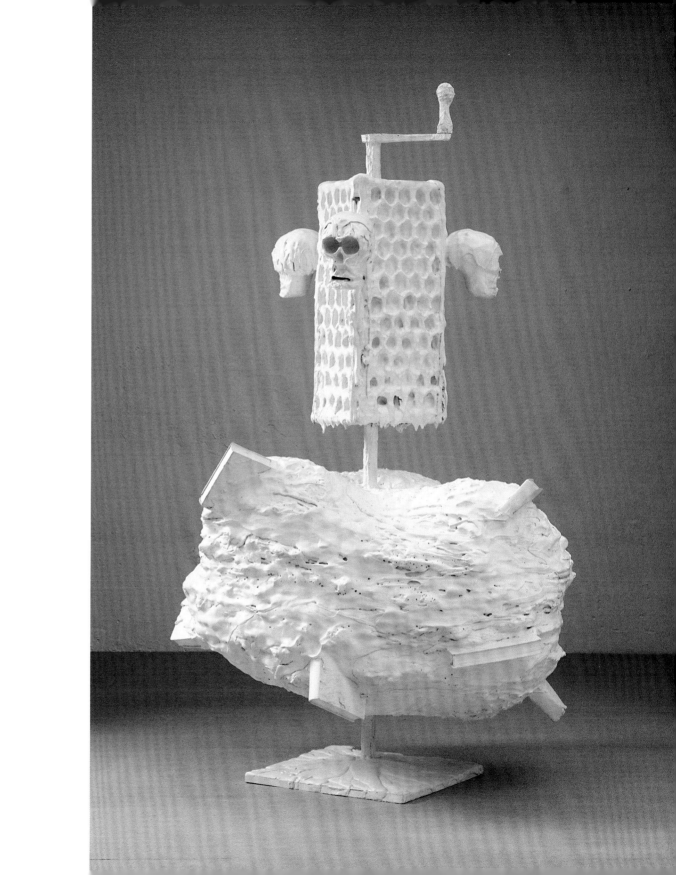

8. **HIVE** 2005

50 × 55 $^1/_8$ × 55 $^1/_2$ in / 127 × 140 × 141 cm
bronze, glass and paint
edition of 8 plus 4 artist's casts

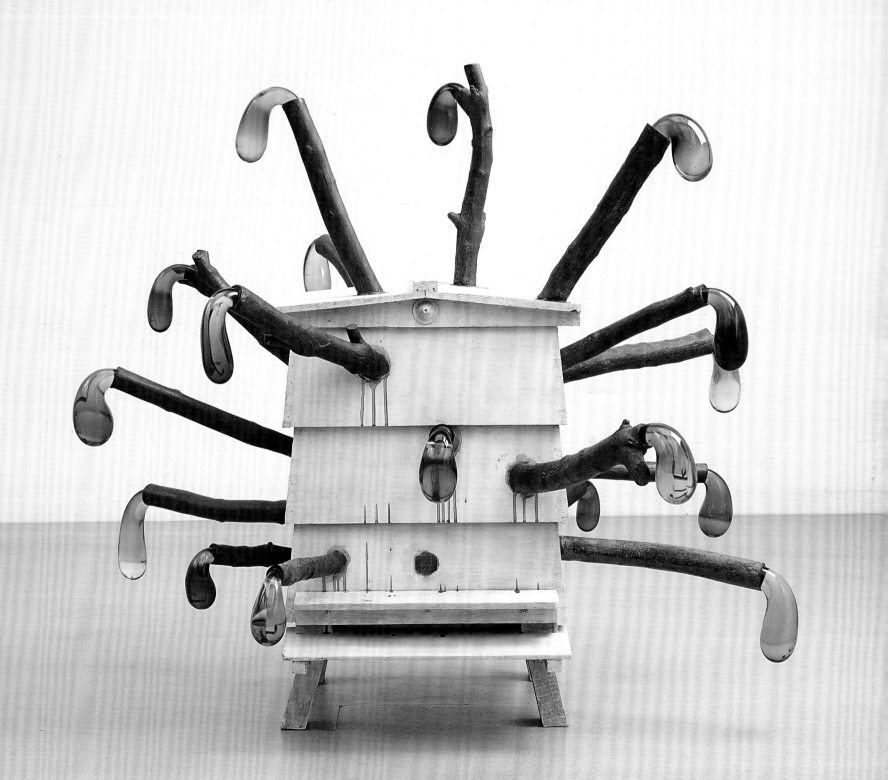

9. **MAQUETTE OF OPEN BOOK** 2005

63 × 30 ³/₄ × 26 ³/₈ in / 160 × 78 × 67 cm
mixed media (to be cast in bronze)
edition of 3 plus 1 artist's cast

10. **MISSILE 2** 2003

6 $^5/_8$ × 7 $^1/_8$ × 4 in / 17 × 10.5 × 10 cm
bronze and paint
edition of 8 plus 4 artist's casts

11. **SKULLSPAWN** 2004

17 × 13 × 13 $^3/_4$ in / 43 × 33 × 35 cm
bronze and paint
edition of 8 plus 4 artist's casts

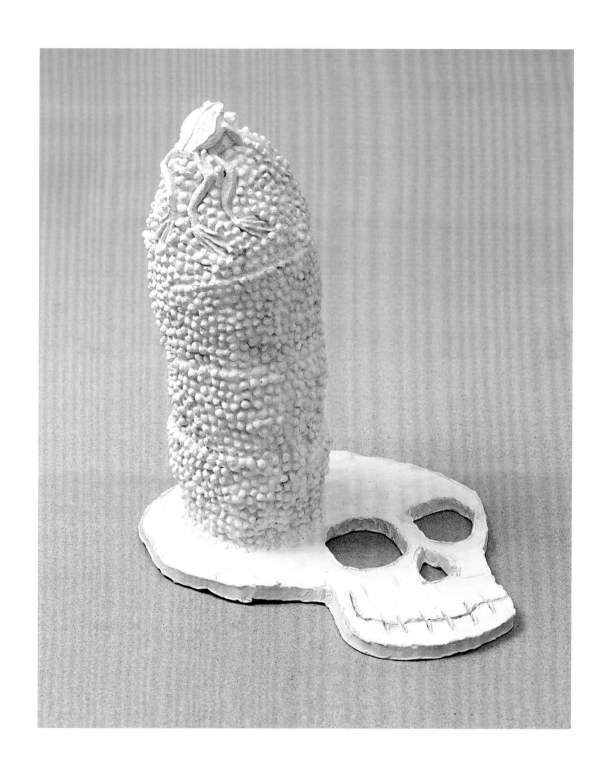

12. **BLACK NAVIGATOR** 2005

18 ¹/₂ × 12 ¹/₂ × 12 ³/₄ in / 47 × 32 × 32.5 cm
ceramic, laminated MDF and gold
unique

13. ULTRAMARINE NAVIGATOR 2005

36 ¹/₄ × 42 ¹/₂ × 41 ³/₄ in / 92 × 108 × 106 cm
ceramic, laminated MDF and gold
unique

14. **KIMONO NAVIGATOR** 2005

19 × 15 $^{3}/_{4}$ × 147 $^{3}/_{4}$ in / 48 × 40 × 375 cm
ceramic, laminated MDF and gold
unique

15. **TERRIL NAVIGATOR** 2005

10 $^3/_4$ × 21 × 6 $^3/_8$ in / 27.3 × 53.3 × 16.2 cm
ceramic, laminated MDF and gold
unique

16. GRAPHITE NAVIGATOR 2005

23 1/4 × 10 × 20 in / 59 × 25.6 × 50.6 cm
ceramic, laminated mdf and gold
unique

17. **CERISE ROUGE NEGOTIATOR** 2005

59 × 118 × 47 ¹/₄ in / 150 × 300 × 120 cm
painted ceramic, laminated MDF and found object
unique

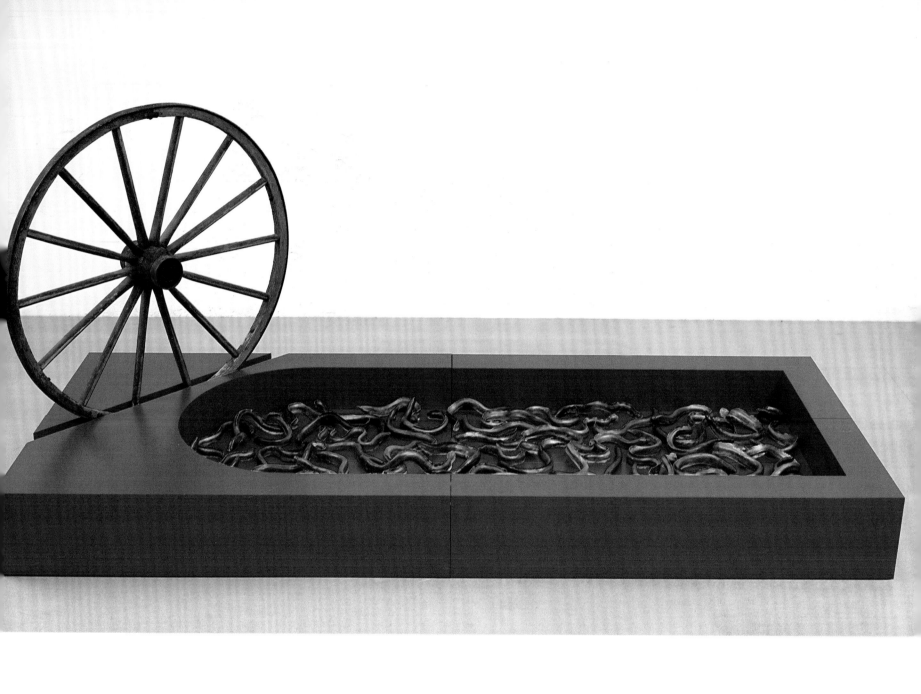

18. SEYCHELLES EVALUATOR 2005

34 $\frac{1}{4}$ × 70 $\frac{1}{2}$ × 46 $\frac{7}{8}$ in / 88 × 179 × 115 cm
bronze, laminated MDF, paint and shellac
unique

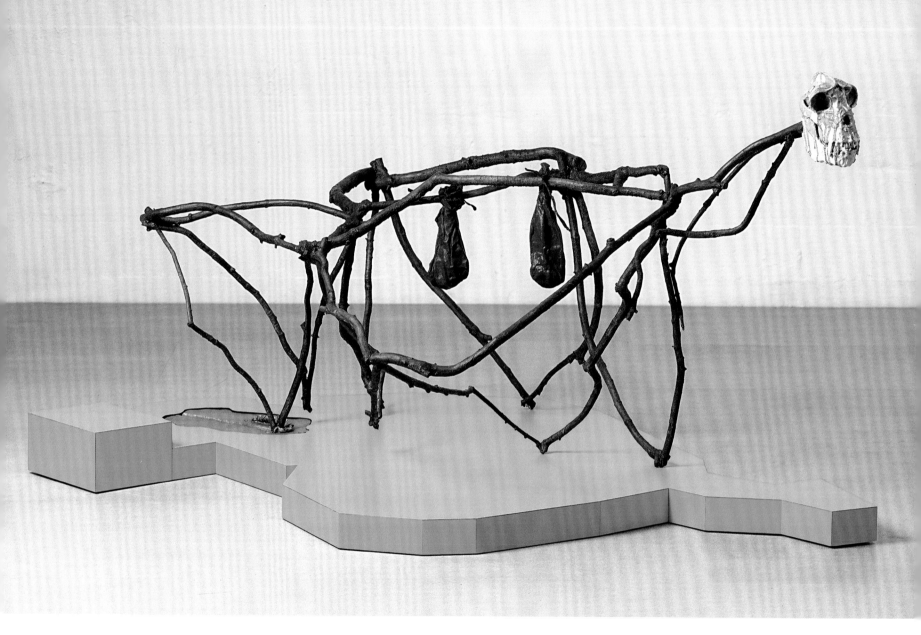

19. DELPHINIUM EVALUATOR 2005

18 $\frac{1}{8}$ × 46 $\frac{1}{2}$ × 39 $\frac{3}{8}$ in / 46 × 118 × 100 cm
bronze, laminated MDF, paint and shellac
unique

20. **CHERRYSTONE EVALUATOR** 2005

26 $^1/_8$ × 58 $^1/_2$ × 28 in / 66.5 × 148.5 × 71 cm
bronze, laminated MDF, paint and shellac
unique

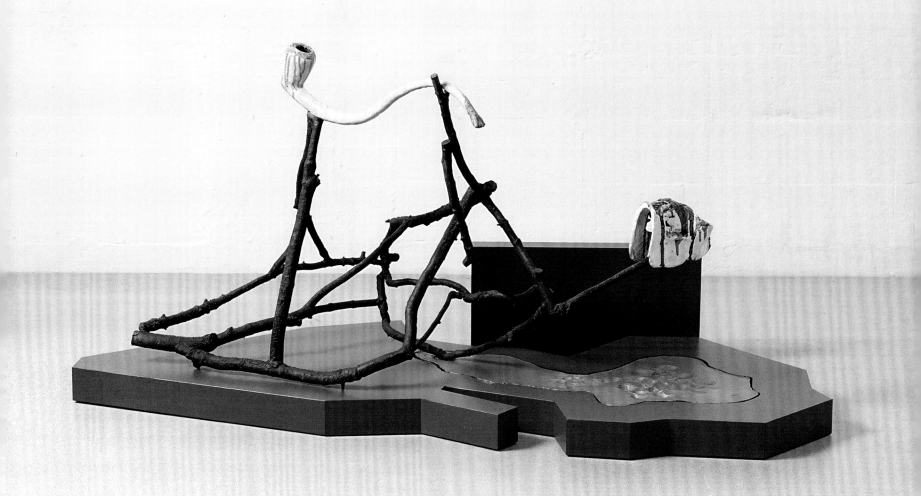

21. **BOYSENBERRY EVALUATOR** 2005

21 $^5/_8$ × 43 × 35 $^7/_8$ in / 55 × 109 × 91 cm
bronze, laminated MDF, paint and shellac
unique

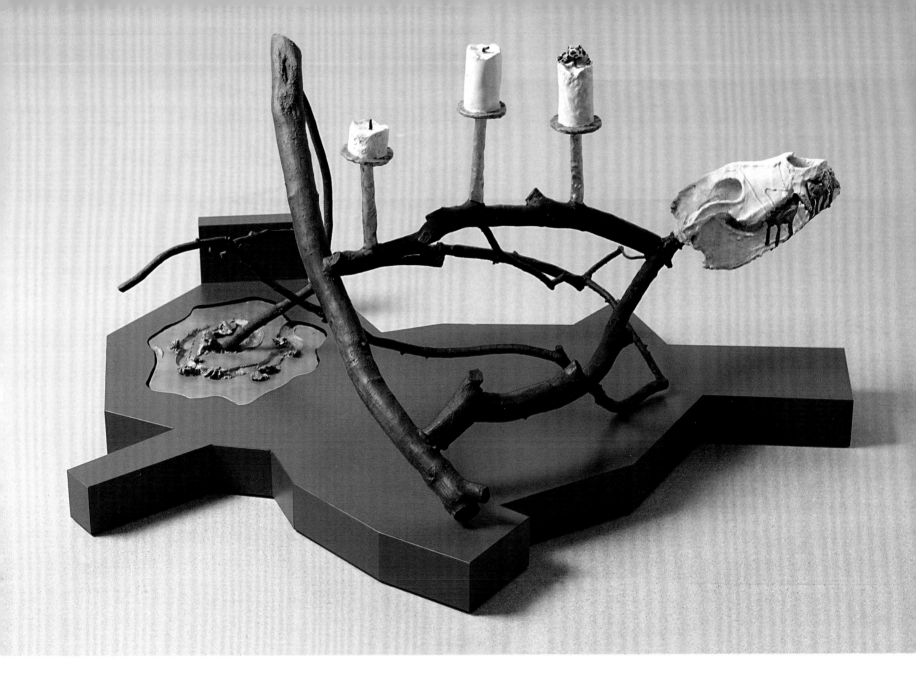

22. HUNTER GREEN EVALUATOR 2005

22 $^7/_8$ × 64 $^1/_2$ × 34 $^5/_8$ in / 58 × 164 × 88 cm
bronze, laminated MDF and paint
unique

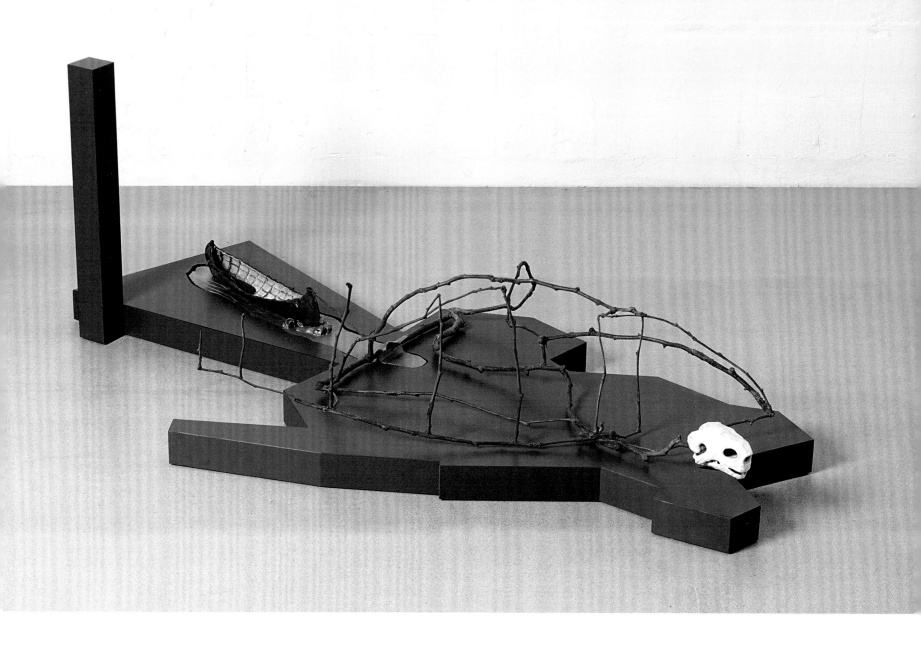

23. **LEAD EVALUATOR** 2005

16 $^3/_8$ × 82 $^1/_4$ × 33 $^7/_8$ in / 41.5 × 209 × 86 cm
bronze, laminated MDF, gold leaf and paint
unique

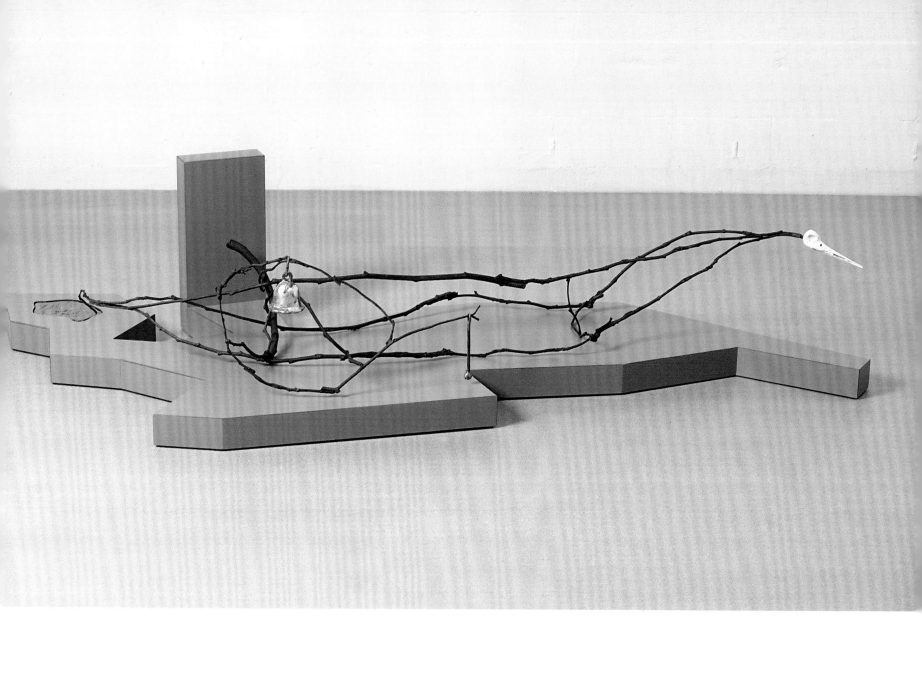

24. **PILLARBOX INVIGILATOR** 2005

63 $^{3}/_{8}$ × 92 $^{1}/_{2}$ × 50 in / 161 × 235 × 127 cm
bronze, laminated MDF, paint and shellac
unique

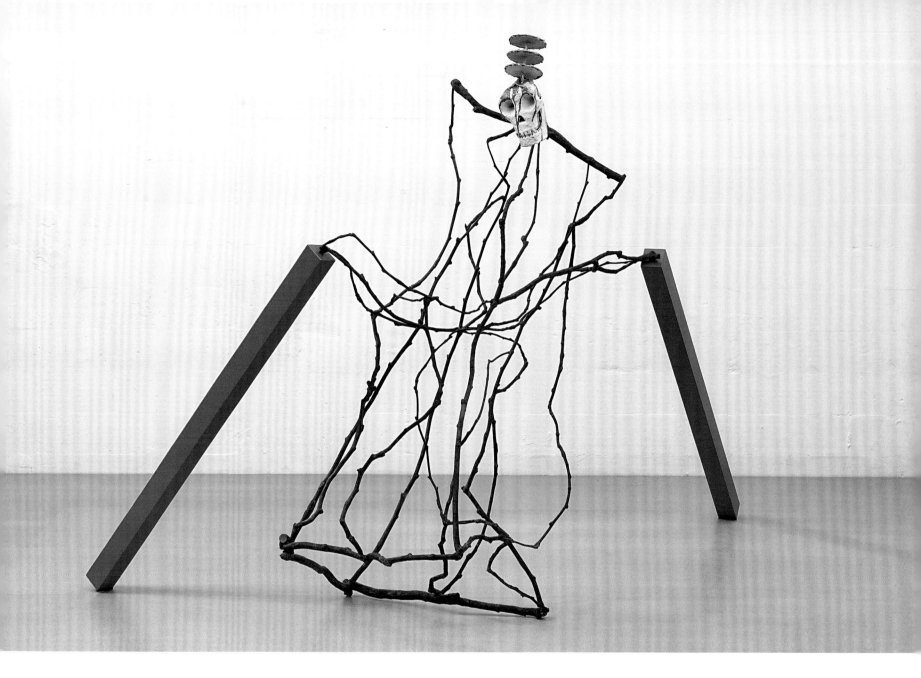

LIST OF WORKS   BIOGRAPHY   EXHIBITIONS

LIST OF WORKS

MDF = medium density fibreboard

1. **VERTICAL PUPA** 1997

   13 $\frac{1}{2}$ × 10 $\frac{1}{4}$ × 7 $\frac{1}{2}$ in / 34.5 × 26 × 19 cm
   bronze, paint and wax
   unique

2. **SUPPORTED PUPA** 1997

   6 $\frac{1}{4}$ × 13 × 9 $\frac{1}{2}$ in / 16 × 33 × 24 cm
   bronze, paint and wax
   unique

3. **KNOTTED PUPA** 1997

   3 $\frac{7}{8}$ × 9 $\frac{1}{2}$ × 13 $\frac{3}{8}$ in / 10 × 24 × 34 cm
   bronze, paint and wax
   unique

4. **GLOBULE** 1997

   39 × 39 × 26 in / 99 × 99 × 66 cm
   bronze, wax, gold leaf, paint, shellac and glass
   unique

5. **SHIP OF FOOLS WITH SMOKER** 2000

   41 × 24 $\frac{3}{8}$ × 20 $\frac{1}{2}$ in / 105 × 63 × 53 cm
   patinated bronze
   edition of 8 plus 4 artist's casts

6. **CELLOSWARM** 2002

   83 × 37 $\frac{3}{8}$ × 37 $\frac{3}{4}$ in / 211 × 95 × 96 cm
   bronze, stone and gold leaf
   edition of 8 plus 4 artist's casts

7. **SEPARATOR 2** 2002

   67 × 42 $\frac{1}{2}$ × 34 $\frac{5}{8}$ in / 170 × 108 × 88 cm
   bronze and paint
   unique

8. **HIVE** 2005

   50 × 55 $\frac{1}{8}$ × 55 $\frac{1}{2}$ in / 127 × 140 × 141 cm
   bronze, glass and paint
   edition of 8 plus 4 artist's casts

9. **MAQUETTE OF OPEN BOOK** 2005

   63 × 30 $\frac{3}{4}$ × 26 $\frac{3}{8}$ in / 160 × 78 × 67 cm
   mixed media (to be cast in bronze)
   edition of 3 plus 1 artist's cast

10. **MISSILE 2** 2003

    6 $\frac{5}{8}$ × 7 $\frac{1}{8}$ × 4 in / 17 × 10.5 × 10 cm
    bronze and paint
    edition of 8 plus 4 artist's casts

11. **SKULLSPAWN** 2004

    17 × 13 × 13 $\frac{3}{4}$ in / 43 × 33 × 35 cm
    bronze and paint
    edition of 8 plus 4 artist's casts

12. **BLACK NAVIGATOR** 2005

    18 $\frac{1}{2}$ × 12 $\frac{1}{2}$ × 12 $\frac{3}{4}$ in / 47 × 32 × 32.5 cm
    ceramic, laminated MDF and gold
    unique

13. **ULTRAMARINE NAVIGATOR** 2005

36 $\frac{1}{4}$ × 42 $\frac{1}{2}$ × 41 $\frac{3}{4}$ in / 92 × 108 × 106 cm
ceramic, laminated MDF and gold
unique

14. **KIMONO NAVIGATOR** 2005

19 × 15 $\frac{3}{4}$ × 147 $\frac{3}{4}$ in / 48 × 40 × 375 cm
ceramic, laminated MDF and gold
unique

15. **TERRIL NAVIGATOR** 2005

10 $\frac{3}{4}$ × 21 × 6 $\frac{3}{8}$ in / 27.3 × 53.3 × 16.2 cm
ceramic, laminated MDF and gold
unique

16. **GRAPHITE NAVIGATOR** 2005

23 $\frac{1}{4}$ × 10 × 20 in / 59 × 25.6 × 50.6 cm
ceramic, laminated MDF and gold
unique

17. **CERISE ROUGE NEGOTIATOR** 2005

59 × 118 × 47 $\frac{1}{4}$ in / 150 × 300 × 120 cm
painted ceramic, laminated MDF and found object
unique

18. **SEYCHELLES EVALUATOR** 2005

34 $\frac{1}{4}$ × 70 $\frac{1}{2}$ × 46 $\frac{7}{8}$ in / 88 × 179 × 115 cm
bronze, laminated MDF, paint and shellac
unique

19. **DELPHINIUM EVALUATOR** 2005

18 $\frac{1}{8}$ × 46 $\frac{1}{2}$ × 39 $\frac{3}{8}$ in / 46 × 118 × 100 cm
bronze, laminated MDF, paint and shellac
unique

20. **CHERRYSTONE EVALUATOR** 2005

26 $\frac{1}{8}$ × 58 $\frac{1}{2}$ × 28 in / 66.5 × 148.5 × 71 cm
bronze, laminated MDF, paint and shellac
unique

21. **BOYSENBERRY EVALUATOR** 2005

21 $\frac{5}{8}$ × 43 × 35 $\frac{7}{8}$ in / 55 × 109 × 91 cm
bronze, laminated MDF, paint and shellac
unique

22. **HUNTER GREEN EVALUATOR** 2005

22 $\frac{7}{8}$ × 64 $\frac{1}{2}$ × 34 $\frac{5}{8}$ in / 58 × 164 × 88 cm
bronze, laminated MDF and paint
unique

23. **LEAD EVALUATOR** 2005

16 $\frac{3}{8}$ × 82 $\frac{1}{4}$ × 33 $\frac{7}{8}$ in / 41.5 × 209 × 86 cm
bronze, laminated MDF, gold leaf and paint
unique

24. **PILLARBOX INVIGILATOR** 2005

63 $\frac{3}{8}$ × 92 $\frac{1}{2}$ × 50 in / 161 × 235 × 127 cm
bronze, laminated MDF, paint and shellac
unique

BIOGRAPHY

1948	Born near Henley, Oxfordshire
1967-68	Winchester School of Art, Winchester
1968-71	St Martins School of Art, London
1971-72	Chelsea School of Art, London
1982	Represented Britain at the Sydney and Paris Biennale
1983	Represented Britain at the São Paulo Biennale
1985	Represented Britain at the Paris Biennale
1986	Finalist, Turner Prize, Tate Gallery, London
1988	Winner of Anne Gerber Award, Seattle Museum of Art, USA
1991	Represented Britain at the São Paulo Biennale
1996-2001	Trustee of the Tate Galleries
2000/01	*Regardless of History*, installed on the Fourth Plinth, Trafalgar Square, London
2002	Elected to the Royal Academy of Arts, London
2003	Elected Trustee of the Imperial War Museum, London
	Elected Governor of the University of the Arts, London

Lives and works in London

SELECTED SOLO EXHIBITIONS

1972
Whitechapel Art Gallery, London

1979
Kunstlerhaus, Hamburg

1980
The Gallery, Acre Lane, London

1981
L.Y.C. Gallery, Banks, Cumbria
New 57 Gallery, Edinburgh
Galerie Wittenbrink, Regensburg

1982
Lisson Gallery, London
Kunstausstellungen, Stuttgart
Galerie Eric Fabre, Paris
St. Paul's Gallery, Leeds
Ray Hughes Gallery, Brisbane
Galerie t'Venster, Rotterdam
Galerie Lachowsky, Antwerp

1983
Galleria Toselli, Milan
Museum van Hedendaasgse Kunst, Ghent
Lisson Gallery, London
Museum of Modern Art, Oxford
Barbara Gladstone Gallery, New York
Locus Solus, Genoa
art and project, Amsterdam

1984
Mercer Union, Toronto
Musée de Toulon, Toulon
Paul Maenz, Cologne

1985
Kunsthalle Basel, Basel
Barbara Gladstone Gallery, New York
Donald Young Gallery, Chicago
La Jolla Museum of Contemporary Art,
California
(*Currents*, I.C.A., Boston)
Matrix, University Art Museum, University of
California, Berkeley

1986
Galerie Nordenhake, Malmo
Paul Maenz, Cologne
Butler Gallery, Kilkenny
Fruitmarket Gallery, Edinburgh
Installation for the Mattress Factory, Pittsburgh

1987
Kunstverein, Munich
Lisson Gallery, London
Cornerhouse, Manchester
Barbara Gladstone Gallery, New York

1988
Paul Maenz, Cologne
Seattle Art Museum, Seattle
Christmas Tree, Tate Gallery, London

1989
Musée des Beaux-Arts, Le Havre; touring to
Musée des Beaux-Arts, Calais
Galerie Nordenhake, Stockholm
Mala Galerija, Moderna Galerija, Ljubljana

Fred Hoffman Gallery, Los Angeles
Saatchi Collection, London
Imperial War Museum, London

1990
Galerie Fahnemann, Berlin

1991
XXI São Paulo Bienal, Brazil
Galleria Locus Solus, Genova
Galerie für Druckgrafik, Zürich

1992
Galerie Sabine Wachters, Brussels and Knokke

1993
Quint Krichman Projects, La Jolla, California
(drawings)
Chisenhale Gallery, London; touring to Aspex
Gallery, Portsmouth (with Richard Deacon)

1994
Galerie Sabine Wachters, Brussels (with Richard
Deacon)
Model Arts Centre, Sligo; touring to Limerick
City Gallery of Art, Limerick
Galerie Sabine Wachters, Brussels and Knokke
(drawings)
Musée Ianchelevici, La Louvière, Belgium

1995
Oriel, Cardiff
Camden Arts Centre, London (drawings);
touring to Harris Museum and Art Gallery,
Preston

1996
Duveen Galleries, Tate Gallery, London; touring

to Institut Mathildenhöhe, Darmstadt, Germany
Ormeau Baths Gallery, Belfast (drawings)

1997
Butler Gallery, Kilkenny (drawings)
Mestna Gallerija, Ljubljana
Galerie Sabine Wachters, Brussels

1998
Galerie Sabine Wachters, Brussels (drawings)

1999
Lothbury Gallery, London

2000
New Art Centre Sculpture Park and Gallery,
Salisbury
Fourth Plinth, Trafalgar Square, London

2000/01
Monographic Room, Tate Modern, London

2001
South London Gallery, London; touring to
Mappin Art Gallery, Sheffield

2002
Glynn Vivian Art Gallery, Swansea

2004
New Art Centre Sculpture Park and Gallery,
Salisbury; touring to Palácio Nacional de
Quelez, Lisbon (with Richard Deacon)

2005
Yorkshire Sculpture Park (with Richard Deacon)
Snape Maltings, Snape, Suffolk

SELECTED GROUP EXHIBITIONS

1971
Art Systema, Museo de Arte Moderno, Buenos
Aires
Art as an Idea in England, C.A.Y.C, Buenos Aires

1972
3rd Biennale of Colombia, Bogota
Platform 72, Museum of Modern Art, Oxford
Drawing, Museum of Modern Art, Oxford

1981
An International Show of Fourteen New Artists,
Lisson Gallery, London
Objects and Sculpture, Arnolfini, Bristol; touring
to I.C.A, London
Through the Summer, Lisson Gallery, London
British Sculpture in the 20th Century,
Whitechapel Art Gallery, London

1982
Biennale of Sydney, Sydney
South Bank Show, South London Art Gallery,
London
Aperto 82, Biennale di Venezia, Venice
Englische Plastik Heute, Kunstmuseum, Lucerne,
Switzerland
XII Biennale de Paris, Paris
Prefiguration, Chambéry, France
London/New York–1982, Lisson Gallery, London
Objects & Figures, Fruitmarket Gallery,
Edinburgh

1983
Tema Celeste, Museo Civico d'Arte
Contemporanea, Gibellina, Italy
La Trottola de Sirio, Centro d'Arte
Contemporanea, Siracusa, Italy
A Pierre et Marie (Phase 1), Rue d'Ulm, Paris
Truc et Troc, ARC Musée d'Art Moderne de la
Ville de Paris, Paris
La Grande Absente, Musée d'Ixelles, Brussels
A Pierre et Marie (Phase 2), Rue d'Ulm, Paris
Australian Perspecta 1983, Art Gallery of New
South Wales, Sydney
Beelden 1983, Rotterdam
Forme e Informe, Bologna
A Pierre et Marie (Phase 3), Rue d'Ulm, Paris
Reseau Art 83, Art Prospect, France
The Sculpture Show, Hayward/Serpentine
Gallery, London
New Art at the Tate Gallery, Tate Gallery, London
Costellazione, Galleria Giorgio Persano, Turin
Transformations, XVIII São Paulo Bienal, Museu
de Arte Moderna, Rio de Janiero; touring to
Museo de Arte Moderno, Mexico City and
Fundação Calouste Gulbenkian, Lisbon
As of Now, Walker Art Gallery, Liverpool;
touring to Douglas Hyde Gallery, Dublin
Skulptur Heute 1, Galerie Joellenbeck/Galerie
Wintersberger, Cologne
La Imagen del Animal, Palácio de las Alhajas,
Madrid
A Pierre et Marie (Phase 5), Rue d'Ulm, Paris

1984
Salvaged, P.S.1, New York
*An International Survey of Recent Painting and
Sculpture*, Museum of Modern Art, New York
Skulptur im 20. Jahrhundert, Merian Park, Basel

Contemporary Acquisitions, Imperial War Museum, London
Terrae Motus 1, Fondazione Amelio, Naples
Home and Abroad, Serpentine Gallery, London
Through the Summer 1984, Lisson Gallery, London
Biennale van de Kritiek 1984, Antwerp
Sculptures dans L'Usine, Comité d'Etablissement Renault Sandouville; touring to Musée des Beaux-Art André Malraux, Le Havre
The British Art Show, City Museum and Art Gallery, Ikon Gallery, Birmingham; touring to Royal Scottish Academy, Edinburgh; Mappin Art Gallery, Sheffield; Southampton Art Gallery, Southampton
Armed, Interim Art, London
Deux Regions en France: L'Art International D'Aujourd'Hui, Palais des Beaux-Arts, Charleroi, Belgium
Opere su Carta 1984, Centro d'Arte Contemporanea, Siracusa, Italy

1985
Space Invaders, MacKenzie Art Gallery, Regina; touring Canada
One City a Patron, Collins Gallery, Glasgow; touring Scotland
The British Show, Art Gallery of Western Australia, Perth; touring to Art Gallery of New South Wales, Sydney; Queensland Art Gallery, Brisbane; Royal Exhibition Building, Melbourne; National Gallery of Art, Wellington
Sculptures du Frac Rhône-Alpes, Musée Sainte Croix, Poitiers; touring France
Nouvelle Biennale de Paris 85, Paris
Drawing: Painting and Sculpture, Brooke Alexander Inc., New York
Recent Acquisitions, Moderna Museet, Stockholm
Social Studies, Barbara Gladstone Gallery, New York
Currents, I.C.A., Boston
Sculptures, Fondation Cartier, Paris
The Irresistible Object: Still Life 1600- 1985, Leeds City Art Galleries, Leeds
1985 Carnegie International, Museum of Art, Pittsburgh

1986
Entre el Objeto y la Imagen, Palacio de Velazquez, Madrid; touring to Centre Cultural de la Caixa de Pensions, Barcelona; Museo de Belles Artes, Bilbao
Sculpture, 9 Artists from Britain, Louisiana Museum, Humlebæk, Denmark
Painting and Sculpture Today, Indianapolis Museum of Art, Indianapolis
Recent Sculpture, BlumHelman, New York
American/European Painting and Sculpture 1986, L.A. Louver, California
The Turner Prize, Finalists Exhibition, Tate Gallery, London

1987
British Sculpture since 1965, Museum of Contemporary Art, Chicago; touring to Peace Museum, Chicago; San Francisco Museum of Art; Newport Harbor Art Museum; Hirshhorn Museum, Washington, D.C.; Albright-Knox Art Gallery, Buffalo, New York
Documenta 8, Kassel, Germany
Conversations, Darlington Arts Centre; touring England
Current Affairs, Museum of Modern Art, Oxford; touring to Mucsarnok, Budapest; Narodni Galerie, Prague; Zacheta, Warsaw
Terrae Motus, Grand Palais, Paris
British Art of the 1980s, Liljevalchs Konsthall, Stockholm; touring to Sara Hilden Art Museum, Tampere, Finland
Art Against Aids, Barbara Gladstone Gallery, New York
Juxtapositions, P.S.1, New York
Documenta 8, Kassel, Germany
20th Anniversary Exhibition, Lisson Gallery, London
Vessel, Serpentine Gallery, London

1988
Starlit Waters, Tate Gallery, Liverpool
Modern British Sculpture from the Collection, Tate Gallery, Liverpool
British Now: Sculpture et Autres Dessins, Musée d'Art Contemporain de Montreal, Montreal
Britannica, Ecole d'Architecture de Normandie, Rouen; touring to Museum van Hedendaagse Kunst, Antwerp; Centre d'Art Contemporain Midi-Pyrenéés, Toulouse

1989
Collection du Frac Bourgogne, Musée des Beaux Arts, La Chaux de Fonds, Switzerland
The Thatcher Years, Flowers East, London
Specchi Ustori, Museo Palazzo Bellomo, Siracusa, Italy

1990
Glasgow Great British Art Exhibition, McLellan Galleries, Glasgow
Great Britain – USSR, The House of the Artist, Kiev; touring to The Central House of the Artist, Moscow
For a Wider World, Ukranian Museum of Fine Art, Kiev; touring to The Central House of the

Artist, Moscow
Dessin d'une Collection, Extrait 17, FRAC Picardie, Amiens, France
Metropolis, Berlin
La Sculpture Contemporaine après 1970, Fondation Daniel Templon, Musée Temporaire, Fréjus, France

1991

The New Patrons, Christie's, London
BBC Billboard Art Project (in conjunction with Mills and Allen)
Arte Amazonas, Museu de Arte Moderna, Rio de Janiero; touring to Museu de Arte, Brasilia; Staatliche Kunsthalle, Berlin; Technische Sammlungen, Dresden; Ludwig Forum für Internationale Kunst, Aachen
Le portrait dans l'Art Contemporain, Musée d'Art Moderne et d'Art Contemporain, Nice

1992

Whitechapel Open, Whitechapel Art Gallery and other venues, London
The Cutting Edge, Barbican Art Gallery, London
Innocence and Experience, City Art Gallery, Manchester; touring to Ferens Art Gallery, Hull; Castle Museum, Nottingham; Kelvingrove Art Gallery and Museum, Glasgow
Des Dessins pour les Élèves du Centre entre des deux Thielles, Le Landeron, Centre scolaire et sportif des Deux Thielles, Les Landeron; touring to Offentliche Kunstsammlung Basel, Basel; Museum fur Gegenwartskunst, Basel
Galerie Sabine Wachters, Brussels and Knokke
Scultori Inglesi: Disegni Di Cragg, Deacon, Houshiary, Kapoor, Woodrow, Galleria Federica Inghilleri, Milan

1993

Declarations of War, Contemporary Art from the Imperial War Museum, Kettle's Yard, Cambridge
Out of Sight Out of Mind, Lisson Gallery, London
Recent British Sculpture, Derby Museum and Art Gallery; UK tour
Sculptures Contemporaines Acquisitions Récentes, Musée des Beaux-Arts, Calais
No More Heroes Anymore: Contemporary Art From The Imperial War Museum, Royal Scottish Academy, Edinburgh

1994

Dessins et Sculptures, FRAC de Picardie, Amiens, France
Back to Basics: a Major Retrospective, Flowers East, London
Sculpture at Goodwood, The Hat Hill Sculpture Foundation, Goodwood
Contemporary Art Tsurugi '94, Tsurugi, Japan
A Changing World: 50 Years of Sculpture from the British Council Collection, State Russian Museum, St. Petersburg
Selections from the Lewitt Collection, Atrium Gallery, University of Connecticut, Connecticut

1995

From Picasso to Woodrow: Recently Acquired Prints and Portfolios, Tate Gallery, London
Contemporary Art Society Collection, Butler Gallery, Kilkenny
Weltkunst Collection, Irish Museum of Modern Art, Dublin
Prints and Drawings: Recent Acquisitions 1991-95, British Museum, London

1996

Un Siècle de Sculpture Anglaise, Jeu de Paume, Paris
Natur?, Kunst-und Ausstellungshalle der Bundesrepublik Deutschland, Bonn
Contemporary Art from the Museum's Collection Imperial War Museum, London
From Figure To Object, Frith Street Gallery/Karsten Schubert Gallery, London

1997

Selected Works from the Collection, Irish Museum of Modern Art, Dublin
Works from the Collection, Museum of Contemporary Art, San Diego
Material Culture: The Object in British Art of the 1980's and 1990's, Hayward Gallery, London
Sexta Bienal de la Habana, Havana

1998

The Janet Wolfson de Botton Gift, Tate Gallery, London
Modern British Art, Tate Gallery, Liverpool
A Space Between, Margarete Roeder Gallery, New York
London Calling, Galleria Nazionale d'Arte Moderna, Rome
A Labour of Love, Pallant House Gallery, Chichester; touring to Stadtische Kunsthalle, Mannheim; Kunstverein Hürth, Cologne; Noorbrandts Museum, Hertogenbosch, The Netherlands; Derby Museum and Art Gallery, Derby
Forjar el Espacio, Centro Atlantico de Arte Moderno, Las Palmas de Gran Canaria; touring to IVAM Centre Julio González, Valencia; Musée des Beaux-Arts et de la Dentelle, Calais

Thinking Aloud, Kettle's Yard, Cambridge; touring to Cornerhouse Gallery, Manchester; Camden Arts Centre, London

1999
Separate Messages, Centenary Gallery, Camberwell College of Arts, London
À l'Heure Anglaise, Musée des Beaux-Arts, Valenciennes, France
Spore: Arti Contemporanee nel Transito Epocale, Cassino, Italy
Animal, Musée Bourdelle, Paris
Size Immaterial, British Museum, London

2000
Global Art Rheinland 2000, Kunsthalle, Dusseldorf
Bronze, Holland Park, London
Seven Print Projects from The Paragon Press, Gimpel Fils, London
XXVII Fidem 2000 Internationale Medaillenkunst, Berlin/Weimar

2001
Field Day, Sculpture from Britain, Taipei Fine Arts Museum, Taiwan
Paper Assets: Collecting Prints and Drawings 1996-2001, British Museum, London
Breaking the Mould, Norwich Castle Museum and Art Gallery, Norwich
Permanent installation at Yongsan Family Park, Yongsan-Gu, Seoul
Close Encounters of the Art Kind, Victoria & Albert Museum, London

2002
The Sculpture Park at the Frederik Meijer

Gardens, Grand Rapids, Michigan
Summer Exhibition, Royal Academy of Arts, London
Thinking Big: 21st Century British Sculpture, Peggy Guggenheim Collection, Venice
Blast to Freeze: British Art in the 20th Century, Kunstmuseum Wolfsburg, Germany; touring to Les Abbatoirs, Toulouse
…From Little Acorns…, Early Works by Academicians, Friend's Room, Royal Academy of Arts, London

2003
In Print, Ljubljana, Slovenia; touring to Hakodate, Japan; Shikoku Island, Japan
Handmade Readymade, MacKenzie Art Gallery, Regina, Canada
Le Cabinet de Jean-Michel Alberola - Le Fait Accompli, FRAC Picardie, Amiens, France
Glad that Things Don't Talk, Irish Museum of Modern Art, Dublin
Summer Exhibition, Royal Academy of Arts, London
Independence, South London Gallery, London
Bright Lights, Big City, David Zwirner Gallery, New York
L'Ètat des Choses. L'Objet dans l'Art de 1960 à Aujourd'hui, Musée des Beaux Arts, Nantes, France
A Bigger Splash: Arte Brittanioa da Tate, Pavilhão Lucas Nogueira Garcez-Oca/Instituto Tomie Ohtake, São Paulo
Sculpture at Goodwood, Creative Space, London
Other Criteria, Henry Moore Institute, Leeds

2004
Turning Points: 20th Century British Sculpture, Tehran Museum of Contemporary Art, Iran

Off the Beaten Track, Longside Gallery, Yorkshire Sculpture Park, Wakefield
Domestic [F]Utility, New Art Centre Sculpture Park and Gallery, Salisbury
With Hidden Noise, The Henry Moore Institute, Leeds
Summer Exhibition, Royal Academy of Arts, London
El Estado de las Cosas. El Objeto en el Arte desde 1960 a Nuestros Dias, Museo de Arte Contemporanea, Vigo, Spain
Tom Bendhem: Collector, Ben Uri Gallery, London

2005
El Estado de las Cosas. El Objeto en el arte desde 1960 a Nuestros Dias, ARTIUM, Vitoria-Gasteiz, Spain
Summer Exhibition, Royal Academy of Arts, London
Effervescence, Musée des Beaux-Arts, Angers, France
Raised Awareness, Tate Modern, London

PUBLIC COLLECTIONS

Arts Council of England
British Council
British Library, London
British Museum, London
Government Art Collection
Imperial War Museum, London
Tate, London
Cecil Higgins Art Gallery and Museum, Bedford
Scottish National Gallery of Modern Art, Edinburgh
Leeds City Art Galleries, Leeds
Henry Moore Institute, Leeds
Southampton Art Gallery, Southampton
University of Warwick, Warwick
Museum van Hedendaagse Kunst, Antwerp, Belgium
Musée d'Art Contemporain, Montreal, Canada
National Gallery of Canada, Ottawa, Canada
MacKenzie Art Gallery, Regina, Canada
Ville d'Angers, France
Musée des Beaux-Arts, Calais, France
Musée d'Art et d'Histoire, Chambéry, France
FRAC Bourgogne, Dijon, France
FRAC Haute-Normandie, France
FRAC Picardie, Amiens, France
FRAC Rhône-Alpes, Lyon, France
Musée de Toulon, France
Butler Gallery, Kilkenny, Ireland
Yongsan Family Park, Yongsan-Gu, Seoul, Korea
Museo Tamayo, Mexico City, Mexico
Museum Boymans van Beuningen, Rotterdam, The Netherlands
Rijksmuseum Kröller-Müller, The Netherlands
Auckland City Art Gallery, New Zealand

National Gallery of Contemporary Art, Oslo, Norway
Fundação Calouste Gulbenkian, Lisbon, Portugal
Malmö Konsthall, Sweden
Moderna Museet, Stockholm, Sweden
Kunsthaus Zürich, Switzerland
Museum of Contemporary Art, Chicago, USA
Indianapolis Museum, USA
Museum of Art, Carnegie Institute, Pittsburgh, USA
Metropolitan Museum of Art, New York, USA
Museum of Modern Art, New York, USA
Museum of Contemporary Art, San Diego, USA
Hirshhorn Museum and Sculpture Garden, Washington, D.C.

For bibliographical information, please refer to http://www.billwoodrow.com

Waddington Galleries would like to thank Richard Deacon
and Bill Woodrow for their contribution to this catalogue.

BILL WOODROW SCULPTURES

22 February – 18 March 2006

Waddington Galleries
11 Cork Street
London W1S 3LT

Telephone + 44 20 7851 2200 / 020 7851 2200
Facsimile + 44 20 7734 4146 / 020 7734 4146
mail@waddington-galleries.com
www.waddington-galleries.com

Monday to Friday 10am – 6pm
Saturday 10am – 1.30pm

Designed by Peter Campbell
Printed by Snoeck-Ducaju, Belgium

All photography Prudence Cuming Associates, London

Published by Waddington Galleries
Co-ordinated by Louise Kybert

ISBN: 0-9549982-2-7

THE HOW AND WHY WONDER BOOK OF
INSECTS

By RONALD N. ROOD
Illustrated by CYNTHIA and ALVIN KOEHLER
Editorial Production: DONALD D. WOLF

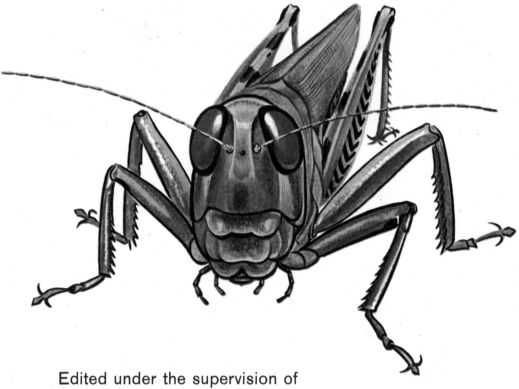

Edited under the supervision of

Dr. Paul E. Blackwood
Washington, D. C.

Text and illustrations approved by

Oakes A. White
Brooklyn Children's Museum
Brooklyn, New York

GROSSET & DUNLAP • **Publishers** • **NEW YORK**

Introduction

We learn in this *How and Why Wonder Book* that there are seven to eight million kinds of insects. How could there possibly be so many? We are sometimes prompted to ask the same thing about the curiosities of children who seem to have endless questions about their world. This book is an ideal source of answers to children's questions about insects.

What is a gold bug? What is a water penny? What is an ant cow? These are just a few of the unusual insects described in the book, along with many more familiar ones.

There is perhaps no more remarkable change in living things than in the development of certain insects from egg to larva to pupa to adult. Understanding this process gives a person a deep appreciation for the remarkable patterns in nature. Seeking accurate descriptions of such patterns is one thing scientists do, and they get great personal satisfaction when they make new discoveries. This book may encourage some children to continue the study of insects, called *entomology,* and select this science as a vocation.

Parents, too, will enjoy this book with their children. In addition to the descriptions of insects, it gives suggestions for an interesting hobby — insect collecting. How to collect, preserve and display them is all told here. Thus, it will prove to be a valuable science reference in the growing list of *How and Why Wonder Books*.

Paul E. Blackwood

Dr. Blackwood is a professional employee in the U. S. Office of Education. This book was edited by him in his private capacity and no official support or endorsement by the Office of Education is intended or should be inferred.

Contents

The Adult Insect

Is a spider an insect? How about a centipede or scorpion? Are crabs and lobsters really big insects that live in the water? Maybe you have seen a tick on a dog, or tiny red mites on plants. Are they insects?

How can you tell an insect from other creatures?

To find the answer, let's look at a good example of an insect — the butterfly. Think of the ways in which the butterfly is different from a spider. First, there are the big wings. Of all the crawling creatures, only insects have wings. Although spiders may sometimes sail through the air at the end of a long, thin, silk thread, like a parachute, no spider can really fly.

Count the number of legs on a butterfly. You'll find that there are six legs. A spider has eight. Crabs and lobsters have ten.

How many legs does an insect have?

Other creatures may have even more. But an insect has just six legs as an adult. Some baby insects seem to have too many legs. Others, like fly maggots, seem to have none at all.

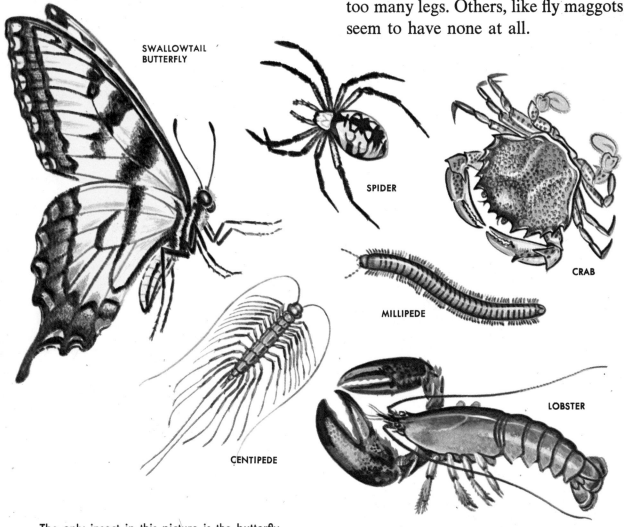

SWALLOWTAIL BUTTERFLY

SPIDER

CRAB

MILLIPEDE

CENTIPEDE

LOBSTER

The only insect in this picture is the butterfly.

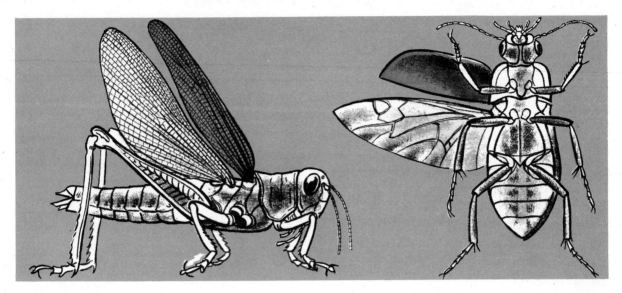

The structure of insects is shown in a side view of a grasshopper and an underside view of a black beetle.

Another way to identify an insect is to count the number of main body parts. Looking at the butterfly, you can see that it has three main body sections:

What are the parts of an insect's body?

(1) A head, with the antennae, or "feelers."

(2) A chest or thorax with all the wings and legs.

(3) A tail-section or abdomen.

The spider seems to have only two parts. Crabs seem to have only one. Scorpions and centipedes have many. And they all have many legs and no wings. So they are not insects.

Why aren't spiders insects?

Not all insects have wings, either. Fleas, some crickets, and even some beetles and moths cannot fly at all. But they still have the right number of legs and body parts as insects—six legs and three main body sections. In fact, the name *insect* comes from a word which means "in sections."

Nobody knows exactly how many kinds of insects there are, but we are sure that there must be more than a million different kinds. Some scientists think there may be seven or eight million kinds — perhaps even more. But we do know that there are more kinds of insects crawling and swimming and flying around than all the other kinds of animals put together.

How many kinds of insects are there?

Each of these insects has its own interesting story. One kind of wasp makes jugs of mud which bake so hard in the sun that they look like stones. Some ants raise plants in tiny gardens. One fly catches a mosquito and lays its eggs on it. Then when the mosquito bites a person, the fly-maggots drop off and burrow under the person's skin.

How are insects different from each other?

There are insects which look like sticks. One of them, the giant walking stick, may be more than a foot long and

5

wider than your finger. It is brown and scaly-looking, like a branch. Its six legs and two antennae look like twigs.

17-year cicada nymphs. Cicadas include 75 species.

Some insects look like plant parts.

How can some insects hide in plain sight? Have you ever chased a bright orange butterfly in the woods? Its colors may be seen many yards away. Just when you think you have it, it disappears. No matter how hard you look, you can't find it. Then it suddenly flies up from right under your feet. If you catch it, then you know why it has been so hard to see. Its bright wings are the color of a dead leaf on the underside. When it folds its wings, the underside is all that shows. It looks like an old brown leaf.

The dead-leaf butterfly looks like the leaves near it.

Many moths can hide in plain sight on the trunk of a tree. Their speckled color is just like that of the bark. A long-legged water bug looks like a floating wisp of hay. Some green insects are shaped just like leaves, while others look like flowers.

One of the most interesting stories is that of the 17-year cicada. It lives seventeen years in darkness below the earth as a nymph. Then suddenly, millions of them come out at once. They leave little holes in the ground about the size of a dime. They cluster so heavily on bushes and trees that the branches bend down with what seem to be large dark berries.

Sometimes insects use tools to help them with their work.

How and why do insects use tools? One wasp picks up a pebble and uses it to pack the ground on top of its eggs. A certain ant uses its babies just as you would use a tube of glue. The ant picks up the baby and presses it against the edges of a curled leaf. The sticky material from the baby's mouth glues the leaf edges together. The ant lion sometimes throws pebbles up into the air so that an insect may be knocked down into its pit — and eaten.

Did you ever forget where you left a hammer or shovel? This couldn't happen to many insects which have their tools with them at all times. The mole cricket has big feet which look like shovels. Burrowing beetles have shovels on the end of their snouts. They are just right for digging the soil. Water striders have waterproof boots in the form of big legs and feet which let them run around on top of the water without getting wet. Diving beetles have a little air-pocket. Then they can breathe under water, like a little skindiver.

The praying mantis has spiny legs which open and close like a jackknife, holding its food tightly. A fly walks upside down on the ceiling because of special pads and hooks which hold it in place. The ichneumon fly has a long drill at the end of its body. With this it can drill deep into a tree trunk to lay its egg in the hole of a wood borer. The tiger beetle has stiff hairs on its feet so it can run over the sand of the beach without slipping.

Bees carry many tools. They have combs and brushes on their legs. These help them work with the wax of the hive. They have a basket to carry the pollen from flowers. Wing-hooks keep their front and hind wings hitched together when they fly. These become unhooked when the bee folds its wings.

You can find inects nearly everywhere you look. Mountain

Where do insects live? climbers find them on high peaks. Explorers bring up blind white crickets from deep caves. Little gray insects called springtails skip about on winter snows. Their dark-colored bodies soak up the warm sunshine and keep them from freezing.

One kind of insect lives right on the edge of Niagara Falls. It is kept from being swept over the falls by a strong thread holding it in place. Other kinds live only in the still water of ponds. Many live inside the stems of weeds. Some fly high into the air, while others spend their lives within a few inches of where they were hatched. If you look at the skin of an orange, you may see some tiny brown scales. These are scale insects, and they don't move at all. Other scales move very little.

Some insects live under rugs and furniture. They may sometimes find their way into your breakfast cereal. Termites and carpenter ants may tunnel through the boards of your house. One little fellow seems to like books. It spends all of its life in libraries.

There is one great place on earth where insects are not found,

Why aren't there any insects in the ocean? and that is the ocean. Insects have never been able to do very well in the seas. Their bodies cannot get used to the salt water. Only a few kinds go into the sea at all, and these stay right near shore. So, even though there are millions of insects, they are crowded close together and fenced in by the oceans that surround us.

Tools that cannot be forgotten:

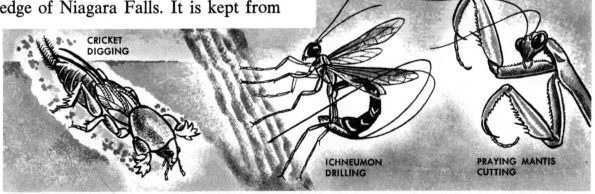

CRICKET DIGGING

ICHNEUMON DRILLING

PRAYING MANTIS CUTTING

Life in a Suit of Armor

What does an insect look like inside? If you cut open an insect, you'd never find any bones, no matter how hard you looked. Its skin is the only skeleton an insect has. Without it, the insect would be soft and helpless.

Flies and mosquitoes have thin skeletons. The beetle looks like a knight in armor with its thick heavy shell. Even soft aphids live in a thin jacket.

How are insects able to touch, smell and taste? If you wore a space suit that covered your hands and face, how would you be able to feel and smell? You would need little holes to sniff through, and other holes for your fingers to feel through. Insects have tiny hairs which

Cutaway view of a grasshopper

poke out through the armor. They also have little pits and pockets. These hairs and pockets help them smell and touch and taste.

Sometimes these pockets and hairs are on the legs of the insect. Many of them are on the feelers or antennae.

They may be on other parts of the body. So we can say that some insects "smell" with many parts of their bodies, instead of just through a nose. In fact, insects don't even have noses at all.

How do insects breathe? Look carefully along the sides of a large insect. Your magnifying glass may show you a row of round circles, looking like the portholes of a ship. These are the breathing pores. They are known as spiracles. Instead of breathing through noses, as we do, insects breathe through holes in their sides.

The spiracles lead to little tubes. These branch all over the inside of the

INSECT SPIRACLE

Bird taking a dust bath

body, even into the legs and eyes. When the insect moves, air is pumped in and out. Even water insects have these tubes. They get their oxygen from the water around them.

Birds take a dust bath to suffocate insect pests in their feathers. The dust clogs up the insects' spiracles, and since they cannot breathe, they die.

When we talk or sing, the noise comes

How do insects "talk"? from our throats. A singing insect makes its noise by buzzing or scraping. Crickets rub their wings together. Grasshoppers rub their legs and wings together. Cicadas have a drum on their bodies. Other insects scratch their bodies or grind their jaws to make a noise. They find each other by following these noises. Sometimes they use the noises to frighten away their enemies.

Katydids have little patches on their

How do insects hear? legs which are sensitive to noises. Grasshoppers have their ears on their abdomen. Some insects can feel sounds or vibrations through their feet, just as you can feel a radio playing by touching it with your fingers. Scientists have not yet found the ears of the champion noisemaker of them all, the cicada. As far as they have been able to discover, it has no ears. It seems to make all that noise for nothing.

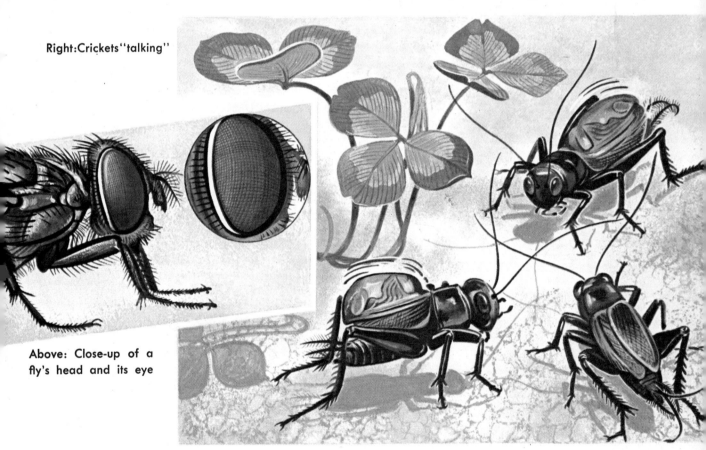

Right:Crickets "talking"

Above: Close-up of a fly's head and its eye

When insects fly, their wings make a humming sound. Sometimes the muscles of the insect make a hum, as well. The higher the hum, the faster the wings are beating. A buzzing housefly beats its wings twenty thousand times a minute.

If you think insects have just two eyes,

How many eyes do insects have? you have guessed too low. What appear to be two eyes are really many small ones packed together. They are called facets.

There may be more than fifty facets

in each of the two large eyes of an ant. One scientist found four thousand in each large eye of a housefly. Some moths and dragonflies may have a total of fifty thousand facets!

For many insects, even this great number does not seem to be enough. They also have a few single eyes right in front of the head. These look like colored beads. They probably help to see things up close, like little magnifying glasses. The big compound eyes help see things farther away.

Even with all these eyes, insects cannot see too well. They **How do insects find their way?** depend mainly on taste and smell. Those little hairs and pits on the body and antennae are very keen. Many male moths have big, feathery antennae which help them find the female in the dark. One scientist found that some moths can find another moth as far as a mile away.

Run a finger across an ant trail to confuse the ants.

10

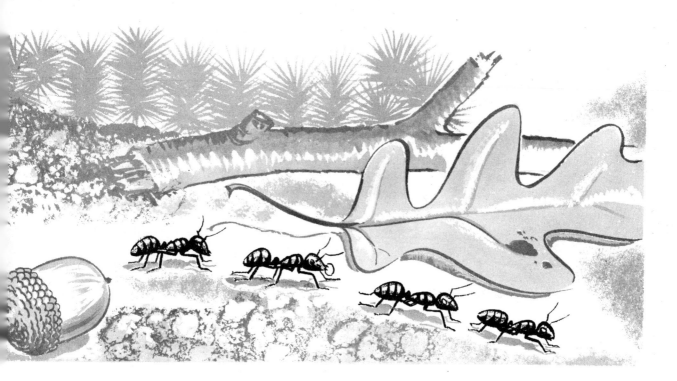

If you have a chance, watch some ants at work. They feel along the ground with their antennae, following definite trails which lead them back to the nest. Each ant follows the trail of the one ahead of it.

Now wipe your finger hard across the trail several times. This will brush away much of the scent. Then watch the next ant that comes along. It stops, turns circles, goes from side to side. It seems completely lost, even if the nest is only a few inches away. It may take three or four minutes for it to find its way again.

One scientist saw a long line of caterpillars. Each was following the one ahead of it. The line went over logs and under bushes, like a little train.

Then he had an idea. He put some of them on the edge of a glass bowl. Around and around they went, following each other's trail in a circle for days and days. They never stopped or climbed down. They just kept on play-ing follow-the-leader until the scientist took them off.

This was more than just a game for the scientist. He was finding out some important things about insects. Other scientists were also studying them.

Scientists found that insects know how to act as soon as they are born. We have to learn to nail boards together, but insects can make perfect homes on the first try. Our parents help us decide what food to eat, but insects usually never see their parents. The hungry babies know what to eat as soon as they hatch. They know how to hide their eggs, and keep out of danger.

How do insects know what to do?

They can do these things because of what we call "instinct." This usually helps the insect meet all its problems. Instinct tells a Japanese beetle to drop to the ground out of sight the minute you touch its twig. Instinct tells a bombardier beetle to wave its abdomen in the air and squirt you with a bad-smelling spray, like a little skunk. Instinct helps a squash bug put its eggs where they will be hidden, and yet near the best food.

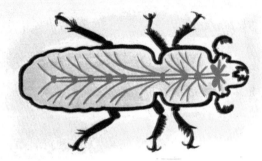

Ganglia (nerve centers) make up an insect's nervous system. They run lengthwise and a double chain of nerves connects them. Nerves branch from each *ganglion* to other parts of the body. The large pair of ganglia in the front is called the "brain."

Instinct is some kind of inner knowledge that helps the insect to do something, although the insect has never been shown how to do it. So instinct may be described as built-in or ready-made knowledge. Scientists, however, don't know what causes it, or how it was made.

Although many insects eat our gardens and forests, some

How do insects help us?

kinds are useful to us. Perhaps you have watched a pair of burying beetles as they dug under a dead mouse until it sank into the ground out of sight. Maybe you have seen ants cleaning up some garbage by taking it into their nest. One kind even carries away cigarette butts.

Ladybird beetles eat plant lice. Some kinds of stinkbugs feed on harmful caterpillars. Water striders keep the water clean by feeding on insects which drop from the bushes. Hornets fly around cows and horses, chasing the flies until they catch one for food.

Perhaps you have seen a painter using shellac. It looks like varnish and is used on boats and airplanes. It comes from the lac insect of India. Some brightly-colored dyes are also made from insects. Silk is made by silkworms to cover their cocoons. The Chinese keep singing crickets in little cages. Even the ground-up bodies of some insects are made into medicine.

Carefully taste a drop of liquid found in the bottom of a flower.

Why do the bees visit the flowers?

It is used by the bees in making honey. When the beekeeper takes the honeycomb from the hive, he always leaves plenty for the bees to eat during the winter. Otherwise they would starve.

When bees go from one flower to another for the sweet nectar they make into food, they also pick up some pollen on the hairs of their body and legs. A

little of this pollen brushes off as they visit each new flower. It helps the flowers' seeds and fruit to grow. Without bees, plants couldn't produce apples, peaches, melons and other good things we have to eat.

Fireflies in a cage make a useful "insect lantern" for the natives of some tropical lands.

Where are insects used for lanterns?

One of the strangest uses for insects is that of lighting a room. In many parts of the world there are no electric lights. When the natives in some tropical countries want to see after dark, they go outdoors with a little cage. They put a few fireflies in the cage. Each firefly has a spot in its body which glows when air is let in through the insect's air tubes. The shining of a dozen large fireflies helps brighten up the room. Some native girls even wear a firefly in their hair.

Fresh Eggs—Handle With Care

INSECTS have many enemies and it is not surprising that they have found many ways to protect themselves. Each one has its own special way of caring for itself.

Even the eggs are given special care by the mother insect.

How are the eggs protected?

How often do you see any insect eggs? If you were able to count all the eggs within a few miles of your house this minute, you would find that there were millions of them. Yet you might look for a long time before you could find any at all.

Some insect mothers bury their eggs deep in the soil. Grasshoppers poke the end of their bodies down as far as they can reach, and lay their eggs in the hole. Some beetles dig down out of sight to lay their eggs. Ants and termites have nests under a stump or in a mound of earth. There the eggs are safely hidden and protected from enemies. Some insects produce a liquid into which they put their eggs. Later, the liquid hardens and the eggs are safe in a covering.

Sometimes you can find insect eggs on leaves and twigs. They

Where can insect eggs be found?

may have tough shells so that other insects cannot eat them. They

Grasshoppers poke their abdomens into the earth as far down as they can reach to lay from 20 to 100 eggs.

may be covered with wax to protect them from winter winds. Perhaps you have seen the egg case of a praying mantis. This fluffy case is like a blanket in the snow. The eggs are safe inside.

You may find a green twig which looks as if someone had been cutting it with a knife. Possibly you will find an insect egg at the bottom of each cut. A cicada makes the cuts with the sharp tip of its body. Then the eggs are safely hidden under the bark.

There are many other places where you can find the eggs of insects. Flies lay their eggs in garbage. Lice attach their eggs to the hair of animals with a special glue of their own. Some walking-stick insects drop thousands of eggs from the trees. It sounds like falling rain. Clothes moths lay tiny eggs in the wrinkles of coats and suits and other cloth garments.

Where do water insects lay their eggs?

Mosquitoes lay large numbers of eggs on the water. Examine the underside of a water lily leaf. You'll find many kinds of eggs. Perhaps you have seen a dragonfly darting along over a pond. It dips down every few seconds to drop an egg beneath the water.

Some damselflies hitch together like a little train. Then the mother fly goes beneath the surface of the water to lay her eggs, while the father fly stays above. When the eggs are laid, the male pulls the female out of the water.

Here is a "damsel train" in action. The female damselfly lays her eggs in the water or else on water plants.

ANGLEWING BUTTERFLY

ATTEVA AUREA MOTH

TAILED BLUE BUTTERFLY

AMERICAN COPPER BUTTERFLY

SWALLOWTAIL BUTTERFLY

ROADSIDE BUTTERFLY

ZEBRA SWALLOWTAIL BUTTERFLY

HAIRSTREAK BUTTERFLY

BUCKEYE BUTTERFLY

FRITILLARY BUTTERFLY

ACHEMON SPHINX MOTH

STRIPED MORNING SPHINX MOTH

BELLA MOTH

ORANGE SULPHUR BUTTERFLY

APANTESIS MOTH

GRACEFUL CLEARWING MOTH

16

One female water bug makes the male bug take care of the eggs. She catches him and lays her eggs on his back!

Some of these eggs are round. Others are flat. Some are brightly colored. Others are wrinkled and brown. Many are black. There are eggs shaped like the crown of a king. Others look like little jugs with pop-up lids. If you have a magnifying glass, you can see various shapes and sizes of insect eggs.

What do insect eggs look like?

Some tent caterpillar eggs take two years to hatch. Fly eggs may hatch in a few hours. Many eggs laid in the fall will not hatch until spring. Some eggs hatch inside the mother insect, so that tiny insect babies are born.

How fast do insect eggs hatch?

MONARCH EGG ENLARGED

This monarch butterfly hides her eggs under a leaf.

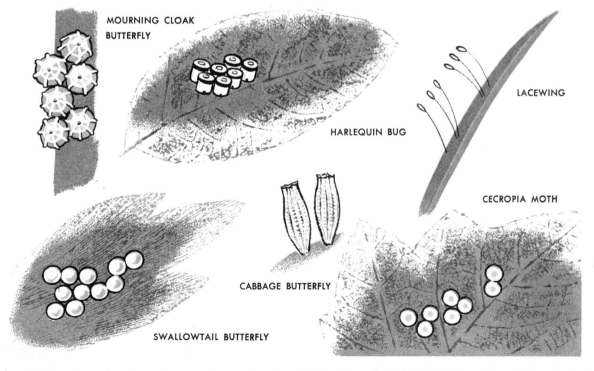

MOURNING CLOAK BUTTERFLY

LACEWING

HARLEQUIN BUG

CECROPIA MOTH

CABBAGE BUTTERFLY

SWALLOWTAIL BUTTERFLY

Insects lay eggs of various shapes, sizes and colors. All the insect eggs pictured here have been enlarged.

A cicada killer buries its victim in an underground passage. The paralyzed cicada has been stung and will provide food for the larva of the cicada killer when the egg hatches later on.

Insect Babies—All Shapes and Sizes

Moths and butterflies lay eggs which hatch out into caterpillars. Big, buzzing bumblebees have little grubs for babies. So do beetles and wasps. Fly eggs hatch into maggots. Caterpillars, grubs and maggots are called larvae.

What are insect babies like?

Grasshoppers and dragonflies have babies which look a lot like the parents. They have little buds where their wings will grow some day. Their heads seem too big for their bodies. These insect babies are called nymphs.

There is one way in which all these different babies are alike. They are nearly always hungry. They begin to eat soon after they hatch, and keep on eating for most of their lives. So the eggs are laid where the insects will have food as soon as they hatch.

How does the mother insect feed her babies?

Perhaps you have seen a wasp pulling and tugging at a caterpillar that had been stung so that it couldn't move. The wasp will poke it down into a new hole in the soil where she has laid her eggs. The new wasp babies will then have food to eat when they hatch.

Some new insect babies are so hungry that they will eat anything at all — even their own brothers and sisters. But the lacewing fly has solved this problem. She lays each egg at the end of a long stalk. When the fierce little baby hatches, it drops off the stalk and begins to hunt for food. Its brothers and sisters are safe on their stalks above.

New baby insects can protect themselves, even in a world filled with hungry enemies. Many of them are the same color as the leaves they eat, so that they are hard to see. Some have fierce-looking spots which make them seem to have great round eyes. Some have sharp spines, making them look like tiny cactus plants.

How do baby insects protect themselves?

One insect puts out a pair of bad-smelling horns when it is in danger. Some insects are long and brown and look just like a twig. Others are round and gray like a pebble. Sharp-jawed ones may pinch you if you bother them. Others curl up and drop into the grass at the slightest touch. Still others are poisonous. Their enemies soon learn not to eat them. Baby insects find protection in their shapes, colors, odors, body poisons and fierce looks.

Most insect babies have no parents to take care of them. **What kind of homes do insect babies have?** The adult insects, their mothers and fathers, usually die soon after the eggs are laid. Wasps, bees, ants and termites, however, take good care of their children. They build nests with many caves and tunnels. Here they have rooms that may be compared to our nurseries, kitchens and storehouses. These nests may be many feet high, and some are twice as tall as a man.

Many baby insects build homes of their own. The caddisfly larva lives on the bottom of streams and ponds. It

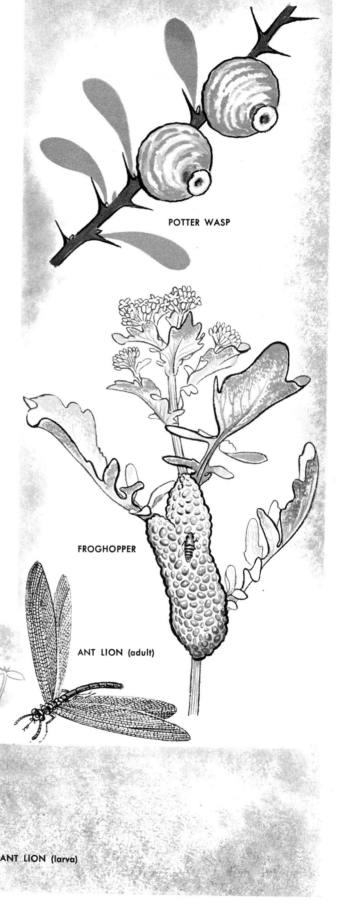

POTTER WASP

FROGHOPPER

ANT LION (adult)

ANT LION (larva)

Insects build nests of many shapes and materials. The ant lion larva below waits for its dinner in a sand pit.

makes a tube of sticks or sand grains glued together. Then it fits itself inside the tube. It looks like a little turtle as it bumps along the bottom of a stream.

One of the strangest homes is the bubble house of the froghopper. You can see many of these nests on grass blades and weeds. If you poke inside the bubbles, you will find a little green froghopper. Put it on a new blade of grass and it will begin to blow bubbles until it is hidden.

The ant lion makes a pit in the dry sand. It waits at the bottom of the pit with its pincers open wide. If an ant stumbles into the pit, the ant lion has its dinner.

Some caterpillars make webs to protect themselves. Other insect babies roll up leaves or cover themselves with dust. Some tiny insects even tunnel in the leaf of a tree, leaving strange marks. Once people thought that the trails of the leaf miners were the writings of ghosts.

The baby insects keep on eating and **Why do baby insects split their skins?** growing. But they don't grow just as we do. An insect's skin doesn't stretch to make more room. It becomes tighter and tighter, like last year's jacket.

One day it splits along the back, and the young insect crawls out of its old skin. Its new skin is soft and thin, and its body swells up quickly. Soon the new skin hardens. Then the insect can no longer grow until after it splits its jacket again.

Only young insects can grow in this way. When the caterpillar turns into a moth, or the grub becomes a beetle, they will never shed their skin again. They stay the same size for the rest of their lives. Little moths don't become big moths, nor little flies big ones.

Some insects are so noisy when they **Does an insect make sounds when it eats?** eat that you can hear them. Perhaps you have heard a scratching sound coming from a wood pile in the forest. It may have been a family of wood borers, a kind of beetle grub. You can often hear them chewing away.

Maybe you have read, in the Bible, about locusts that attacked crops in ancient times, or in the newspapers, about locust attacks in more recent years. Millions of locusts eating a field of grain can be heard some distance away. They sound like the wind in dry leaves.

A cricket or beetle grub chews its food. But some insects sip their food quietly through a long tube. They drink the sap of plants or the blood of animals. If you look where their mouth should be, all you see is a long, pointed tube. Think how it must be to go around with your mouth shut tight and just a straw sticking out!

Who eats more food — you or your **How much does an insect eat?** parents? Many growing insects eat much more than their mother and father eat together. They may eat more than their own weight in food each day. They are growing so fast that they never seem to get enough food.

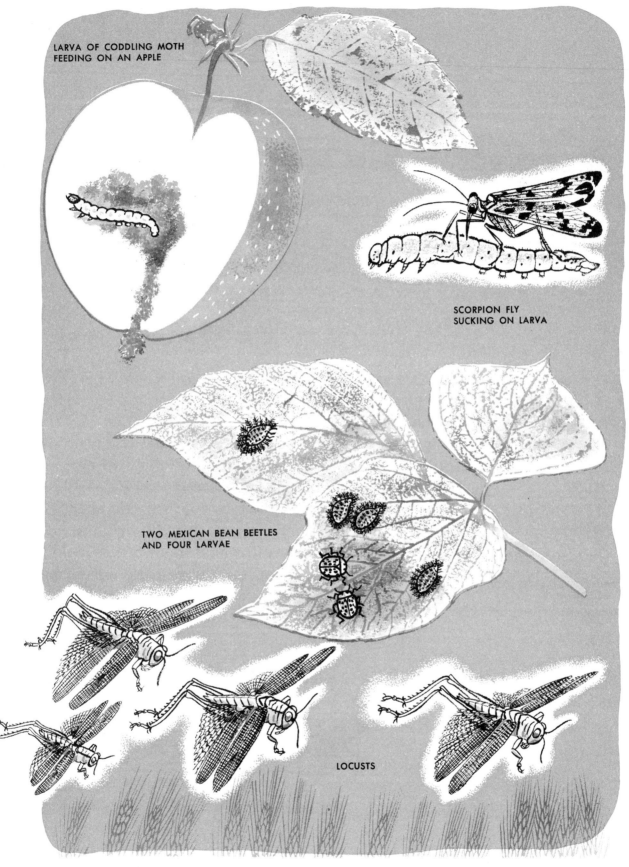

LARVA OF CODDLING MOTH
FEEDING ON AN APPLE

SCORPION FLY
SUCKING ON LARVA

TWO MEXICAN BEAN BEETLES
AND FOUR LARVAE

LOCUSTS

Insects are big eaters. Not only do they feed upon plants, fruit and other insects, but they also feed on woolens, leather, fur, furniture and even books. Locusts are great crop destroyers. Fortunately, birds feed upon them.

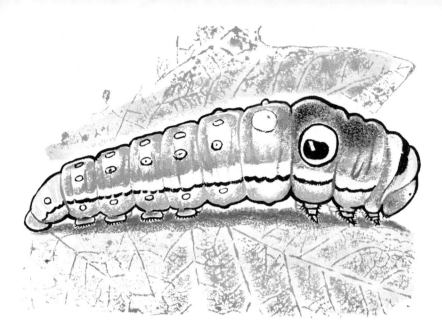

A spice-bush swallowtail caterpillar

The Unlucky Caterpillar

HAVE you ever watched a caterpillar on the sidewalk? Maybe you've seen it chewing on some leaves. If you have a garden, perhaps you have helped spray the plants so it wouldn't eat them.

When the caterpillar eats leaves that have been sprayed with a poisonous chemical, the poison may kill it. At least, the poisonous chemical will cause it to move away.

The caterpillar has been in danger ever since its butterfly-mother first laid her eggs. No matter how carefully the eggs are hidden, other insects come along looking for tiny bits of food, and often find them. Storms and cold weather kill many caterpillars in the eggs, too.

What are the caterpillar's enemies?

When the egg hatches, insects and spiders are waiting for the caterpillar's

Birds are one of the caterpillar's main enemies and help to control many kinds of insect pests.

22

CECROPIA MOTH (adult)

COCOON

LARVA SPINNING COCOON

LARVA MOLTING

Illustrated here is the life cycle of a cecropia moth.

appearance. Birds look at every leaf and twig, eating every caterpillar they can find. Snakes, lizards, toads and frogs catch more of them. And when you go out in the field to make an insect collection, you will catch some, too.

Look at the head of the next caterpillar you find. It seems **Can it see its enemies?** to have two great round eyes in front, but they're not eyes at all. The real eyes are little pinpoint dots which can hardly be seen. It can see only a few inches ahead. Probably the only way the caterpillar

LARVAE EATING

LARVAE GROWING LARGER

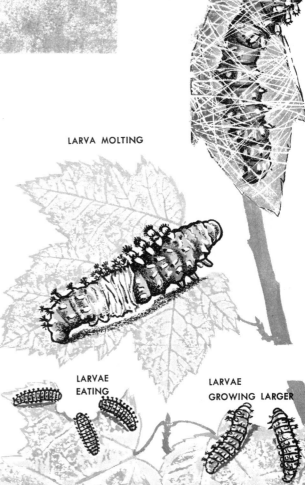

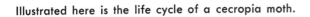

EGGS

LARVAE HATCHED FROM EGGS

knows danger is near is when the leaf shakes as a bird lands near it, or when it smells the scent of a nearby enemy.

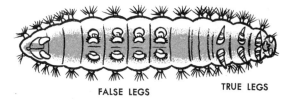

FALSE LEGS   TRUE LEGS

This bottom view of a caterpillar shows its true and false legs. The temporary prolegs will be shed later.

How many legs has a caterpillar? A caterpillar's body is divided into thirteen ringlike parts (segments). Attached to the three segments nearest the head, in the thorax body section, the caterpillar has six little, stubby legs. It also has a few extra pairs of legs along the sides of the segments which make up the abdomen body section. These false legs, called prolegs, are temporary and the caterpillar will shed them along with the last skin.

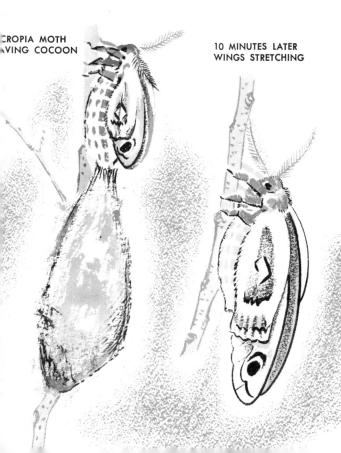

CROPIA MOTH ~VING COCOON

10 MINUTES LATER
WINGS STRETCHING

Why does it eat all the time? You may like a snack after school, or just before going to bed, but the caterpillar is always hungry, and eats almost all day and all night. It needs a great deal of food because it is growing so fast. So it keeps munching on the turnips and radishes in the garden. If the caterpillar has to go without food for more than a few hours it will starve.

What is "molting"? As a caterpillar eats, it continues to grow. However, like other insects, the caterpillar's skin doesn't grow as the rest of its body does. It remains the same size so that, finally, the tight skin splits. The caterpillar then sheds its skin by wriggling out, a process that is called "molting." But underneath is another skin. The caterpillar will outgrow this one, too. In fact, it will molt several times until it reaches the end of the caterpillar stage, and is fully grown.

What is a pupa? After it molts for the last time, the caterpillar becomes a pupa. This is the stage when it goes down into a hole in the earth, or attaches itself to a leaf on a tree. Sometimes it spins silk

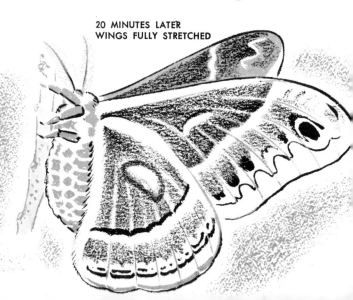

20 MINUTES LATER
WINGS FULLY STRETCHED

threads about itself until it looks like a bit of fluff. This is called a cocoon, the name most people use when they refer to the pupal stage. Maybe you can find a pupa if you look under old boards, leaves or stones.

You'd think it would be safe in the hard pupal shell. But mice nip at pupas with their sharp teeth. Skunks and raccoons dig them up. Even big, shuffling bears tear old stumps and logs apart until they find them.

Finally the great day comes when the pupal stage is over. For **What does it look like when it is full-grown?** some insects, it is only a few weeks, but for most insects, the pupal stage usually lasts the whole winter. Then, in the spring, the pupal shell cracks open and out crawls the insect. It is no longer a caterpillar, however. Now it is a moth, or a butterfly with shining wings. The butterfly spreads its wings to dry in the sunshine. Then it flies away, leaving the pupal shell behind.

If larvae have so many troubles, how can there be so many butterflies and bees and other insects in this world? The answer is one of Nature's most wonderful stories.

Insects develop in any one of three different ways. At the top is the life cycle of a silverfish. This insect looks like its parents as soon as it hatches from the egg and grows gradually until it reaches adult size. This is called gradual development. In the center is the life cycle of the dragonfly which has an incomplete metamorphosis or development. *Metamorphosis* means "change of form." The butterfly shown below has a complete metamorphosis. Its life cycle includes four stages — the egg, larva, pupa and adult stage.

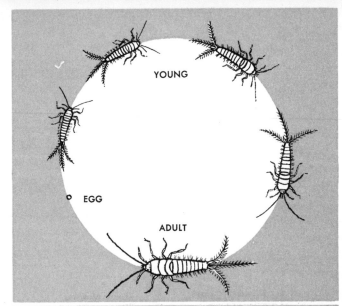

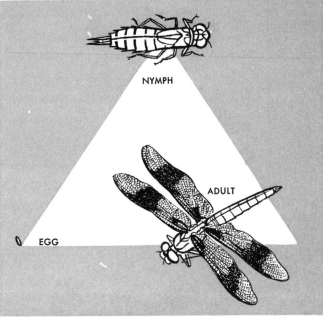

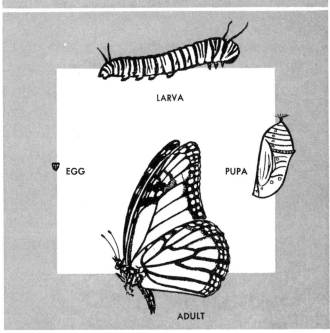

House of Mystery—the Pupa

If you find a pupa or silk-wrapped co-coon, look at it carefully. It's hard to know just what it will be when it hatches out. But if your eyes are sharp, you'll see wrinkles and folds where the new wings will be. You can find the eyes, the mouth and the legs. But unless you see it twist or turn, it seems more dead than alive.

What is going on inside the pupa?

Inside the pupa, there's a wonderful change taking place. Instead of stubby little baby legs, there are the strong new legs of the adult. Folded wings are waiting to spread in the sun. Big round eyes and long antennae are getting ready to help it find its way in the world. The head, mouth and body are all different. No matter how hard you looked inside a pupa, you couldn't find the caterpillar or grub any more.

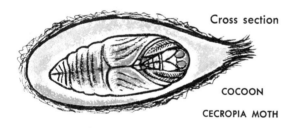

Cross section

COCOON

CECROPIA MOTH

Think of all the changes you'd have to make in order to turn into a bird. You'd have to grow feathers, a beak, wings and claws. All the time you were changing, you'd be wrapped up so tight you couldn't move. This is about what an insect has to do as it changes from a pupa to an adult. No wonder it

Why is the pupa so carefully hidden?

is hidden deep under a log or curled up in a leaf, where it's safe!

SILKWORM COCOON

Do all insects go through this great change? Most of them do, but not those which hatch out of their eggs looking like their parents. Praying mantis nymphs change slowly until they become adults. So do cockroach and squash bug nymphs. Each time they split their skin and grow a new one, they look more like the adult, so they do not need any pupal stage.

Do all insects have a pupa?

SWALLOWTAIL BUTTERFLY PUPA

Some insects anchor the pupa in place with a strong thread. Then, when they pull themselves out later, the old brown shell will stay in place. Other insects seem to do as well without an anchor. Some black flies anchor the pupa under water. They also have a little bubble. When they break out of the pupal case, they ride to the surface in the bubble. When the bubble bursts they fly away.

Why do some pupas have an anchor?

Mourning cloak larva (left) changing to pupal stage.

Jack Frost Arrives

The temperature of an insect changes according to the weather in the insect's surroundings, so that its temperature is always changing.

What is the temperature of an insect?

In the winter, the insects hidden in the ground and under the bark of trees are just about as cold as the snow. They are so cold that they can hardly move at all. In the summer, they are nearly as hot as the sunshine. Then they run and fly very quickly.

If you listen to a cricket chirping, you can guess the temperature outdoors. The warmer the day, the faster the song. One kind, the snowy tree cricket, sings the same musical note over and over. Count the number of times it sings in fifteen seconds. Then add forty. The resulting number will approximate the reading on a thermometer.

You might think that because insects get so cold in winter, you would want to bring them all in by the fire where it is warm. But if they were kept alive and active in a warm house they would starve to death without any food. So it is better that they spend the winter months outdoors. There they just remain quiet until spring comes again.

How do insects spend the winter?

Sometimes they come out on a warm day. Then you see flies buzzing around the sunny side of a house. Sometimes you see caterpillars crawling slowly on the bark of trees. The mourning cloak butterfly often comes out on a sunny January day. It looks quite out of place sailing over the patches of snow.

Insects may spend the winter as a pupa or larva. Other insects lay their eggs during late summer and then die. The only thing that keeps them from dying out completely is the cluster of eggs. Like tiny seeds, they wait for spring. Then, sure enough, they hatch out. They grow up to be just like the parents they never saw.

A few insects are active all year, even where the winters are cold. Lice and fleas which live on birds and animals keep warm in the thick fur and feathers. Cave insects crawl around as usual, for the temperature hardly changes at all inside a cave.

How can some insects keep warm in the winter?

Even on a winter day when the temperature is far below zero, and snow and ice are everywhere, bees are active in their hives. If you should visit an apiary

The fur of a monkey is a warm hiding place for insects.

27

(a place where bees are kept) on a winter day, put your ear against a beehive and listen. You will hear a faint humming sound. Inside the hive, even on a cold day, bees move around slowly, buzzing their wings. This activity keeps them warm enough so that they won't freeze.

A warm beehive sometimes attracts mice and other animals. If a mouse finds the hive, it may eat some of the honey the bees have stored for food. It may build its nest in front of the entrance so that the bees cannot get out in the spring.

Often the bees drive the mouse away with their stings. Sometimes they sting it so much that it dies. Then they have to leave the body there. But the bees often cover a dead mouse with their wax, sealing it up so that the air in the hive will stay fresh.

A few insects go south in the winter, just as the birds do. The big orange-and-black monarch butterfly may travel from Canada to Mexico. It goes in flocks of thousands. Sometimes it crosses many miles of water over the Great Lakes and the Gulf of Mexico. Nobody yet knows how it finds its way. It is one of the greatest of all insect travelers.

Are there any insect travelers?

The mouse has a sweet tooth, especially for honey, but bees know how to defend their property from enemies.

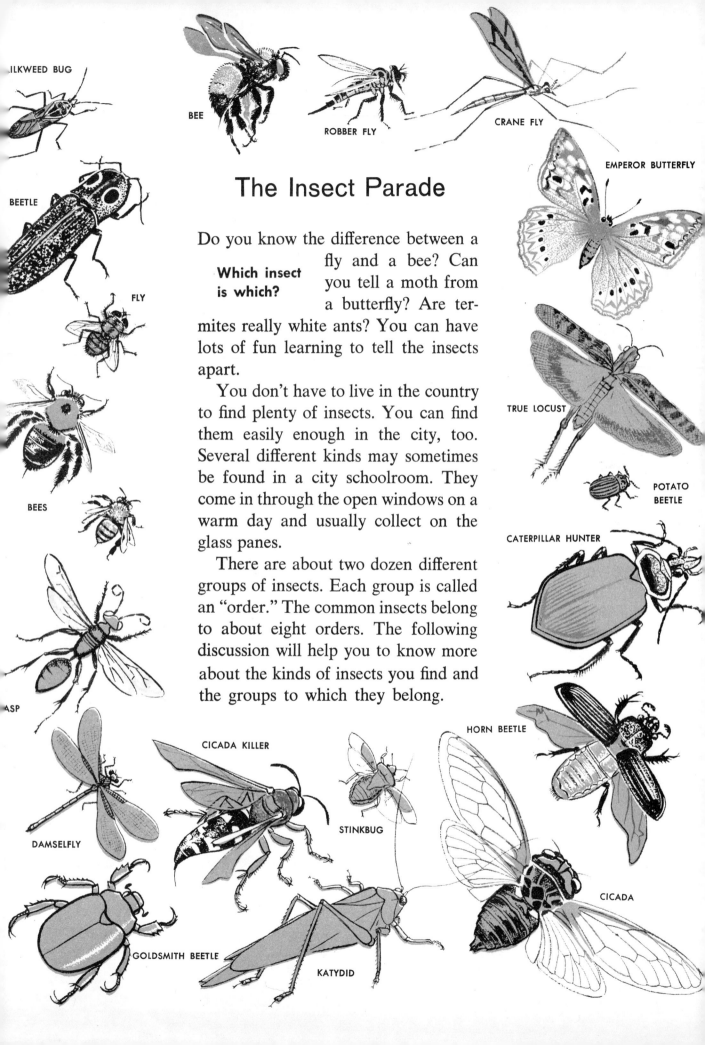

ILKWEED BUG

BEE

ROBBER FLY

CRANE FLY

EMPEROR BUTTERFLY

BEETLE

FLY

TRUE LOCUST

POTATO BEETLE

CATERPILLAR HUNTER

BEES

ASP

HORN BEETLE

DAMSELFLY

CICADA KILLER

STINKBUG

CICADA

GOLDSMITH BEETLE

KATYDID

The Insect Parade

Which insect is which?

Do you know the difference between a fly and a bee? Can you tell a moth from a butterfly? Are termites really white ants? You can have lots of fun learning to tell the insects apart.

You don't have to live in the country to find plenty of insects. You can find them easily enough in the city, too. Several different kinds may sometimes be found in a city schoolroom. They come in through the open windows on a warm day and usually collect on the glass panes.

There are about two dozen different groups of insects. Each group is called an "order." The common insects belong to about eight orders. The following discussion will help you to know more about the kinds of insects you find and the groups to which they belong.

A praying mantis sits upon a leaf that it will soon eat.

1. Relatives of Grasshoppers

The praying mantis is the terror of the

What are some relatives of the grasshoppers?

insect world. It catches and eats nearly every kind of insect it can find. It belongs in this group.

The walking stick is also a relative of the grasshoppers. So are the cockroaches.

Walking sticks eat plant leaves and twigs, but cockroaches eat nearly anything. Cockroaches have even eaten the glue from the backs of postage stamps.

Crickets and grasshoppers are the most

Which are the "music makers"?

musical of insects. They make most of the insect

sounds you hear in the country. The mole cricket even sings under the ground. Locusts buzz their wings together as they fly, and katydids call from the treetops at night.

2. The Dragonflies

Walk near a swamp or brook in sum-

Why were dragonflies called "darning needles"?

mer, and you may see many dragonflies. People used to think they would sew up your ears

while you were asleep. They called them "darning needles." Of course, they don't do any such thing. They are really helpful insects, for they catch thousands of mosquitoes.

If you catch a dragonfly, notice its large eyes and funny legs. The eyes help it to see in almost every direction. The legs form a basket to catch other insects as it flies along. With its wings pointed out to the side, it looks like a small airplane.

Damselflies look like dragonflies and belong to this group. They fold their wings and point them up in the air.

Pictured above is a termite family in its nest. At the top left is the male, underneath is the queen and at

The nymphs of some dragonflies can

How are young dragonflies jet-propelled?

travel by jet propulsion. They squirt water out of the end of their bodies. This makes them shoot forward like a little jet airplane. Perhaps it's more like a submarine, though, for they live under the water.

3. The Termites

If you live in Canada or the northern

How do termites differ from ants?

United States, you may not have seen many termites. They are much more common farther south.

Sometimes termites are called "white ants," but they are really not ants at all. Ants have a thin waist between the thorax and abdomen. Termites are thick-bodied from head to tail.

Soldier termites guard the nest from ene-

What is a termite family like?

mies with their powerful jaws. Hundreds of workers build the nest and get the food. The queen lays great numbers of eggs. Sometimes there may be more than one queen, and a few kings as well.

Sometimes you see termites by the thousands as they come out on a window sill or old stump. These are dark-colored kings and queens ready to leave the nest. They fly to a new spot

her side, a soldier, then the king and workers. At the far right are the mounds of some tropical termites.

and then do a strange thing. They break off their wings so they can never fly again. Then they burrow into the ground and start a new colony.

Termites eat nearly everything made

What do termites eat?

out of wood, leaving only a thin outer layer. Once a teacher opened an old desk drawer. Termites had drilled up through the floor and into the desk leg. They had hollowed out the wood of the desk until it was just a shell. When he pulled on the drawer, the desk toppled.

4. The True Bugs

Not all insects are bugs. The only real

Is every insect a bug?

bugs are those with the soda-straw mouths made for poking into plants or drinking the blood of animals. Bugs have four wings or no wings at all. Half of the wing is tough, like a beetle's. The other half is thin, like that of a fly.

Squash bugs, bedbugs and stinkbugs are all true bugs. So is the diving water boatman with its long legs, which look like oars. Ladybugs and June bugs are not really bugs at all. They are beetles with chewing mouths.

The noisy cicada is a relative of the bugs. So are the green aphids.

Aphids are interesting because they give

Why do ants keep "cows"?

off sweet honeydew which ants love. Some ants even carry aphids down into the ground to feed on the roots of plants. Then they

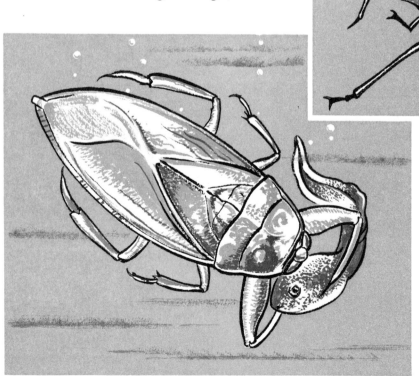

A giant water bug makes a meal of a tadpole. The insert shows a close-up view of a water bug's head and mouth.

have a honeydew supply right in the nest. This is almost like a farmer who keeps cows for milk. So we may say that ants keep aphids as "cows."

Cornfield ants "milking" aphids

5. The Beetles

There are more kinds of beetles than

How many kinds of beetles are known?

any other insect group in the world. If you began collecting beetles at the rate of one new kind every day, your life wouldn't be long enough to collect all of them. It would take seven hundred years. There are more than 250,000 known kinds.

Sprinkle some salt in your hand.

There are beetles so small that they could hide beneath a single grain of salt! There are beetles so large that when they spread their legs they would cover half this page!

Perhaps you remember the Bible story of

Which is one of the largest beetles?

David and Goliath. One of the largest of all insects is the Goliath beetle. It has a body almost as long as a banana. In fact, when a living specimen was sent to a museum, scientists found that it

(Above): Close-up of the head of a male stag beetle.

(Right): Stag beetles, male (top) and female (bottom).

liked to eat bananas. It was found in Africa, and was quite lucky to stay alive long enough to reach America. Some natives in Africa like to fry the giant grubs in oil for food.

You can usually identify a beetle easily

How can you tell a beetle from other insects? when you see it. It has powerful jaws for chewing. Heavy wings look like two shields on its back. Underneath are the folded wings which are used in flying. The wings of the Goliath beetle may spread eight inches.

Stag beetles have jaws so large they look like the antlers of a tiny deer. Ground beetles have powerful jaws for eating other insects. The jaws of the boll weevil are out at the end of a long snout. It looks like a true bug at first, but if you look close you'll see its jaws.

6. The Moths and Butterflies

Rub your finger gently on the wing of

Why are moths and butterflies called "scale-wings"? a butterfly or moth. You will find that a soft powder comes off. A microscope would show you that this powder is really thousands of tiny scales. They are arranged on the wing like shingles on a roof.

Some moths are not much larger than a

How large are moths? pinhead. The largest may have a wingspan of more than a foot. Some are the most colorful of all insects. They may shine bright blue in one light, green or purple in another.

These insects have a coiled tube for

How do moths eat? sipping liquids instead of the pointed beak of the bugs or the jaws of the beetles. They poke this tube down into flowers to get the sweet nectar.

One time several butterflies, near a group of soldiers standing at attention, flew from one soldier to another. They alighted on each bright-colored shoulder patch and uncoiled their long tubes. The soldiers must have looked like some new flower to the butterflies.

Some moths are helpful to man. We un-

Are moths helpful to man? wind the silk from the silkworm's cocoon. Many caterpillars eat troublesome weeds. But many butterflies and moths have babies which are not so helpful. They eat our gardens, our clothes and our forests. Gypsy moth caterpillars may eat the leaves from hundreds of trees at once.

Look at the way a moth holds its wings.

How can you tell a moth from a butterfly? The wings lie down flat over the moth's sides and back. A butterfly holds them pointed up over its back. Moths have antennae which look like feathers. The antennae of a butterfly look like long threads with a knot at the end. And, of course, you usually see moths at night and butterflies during the day.

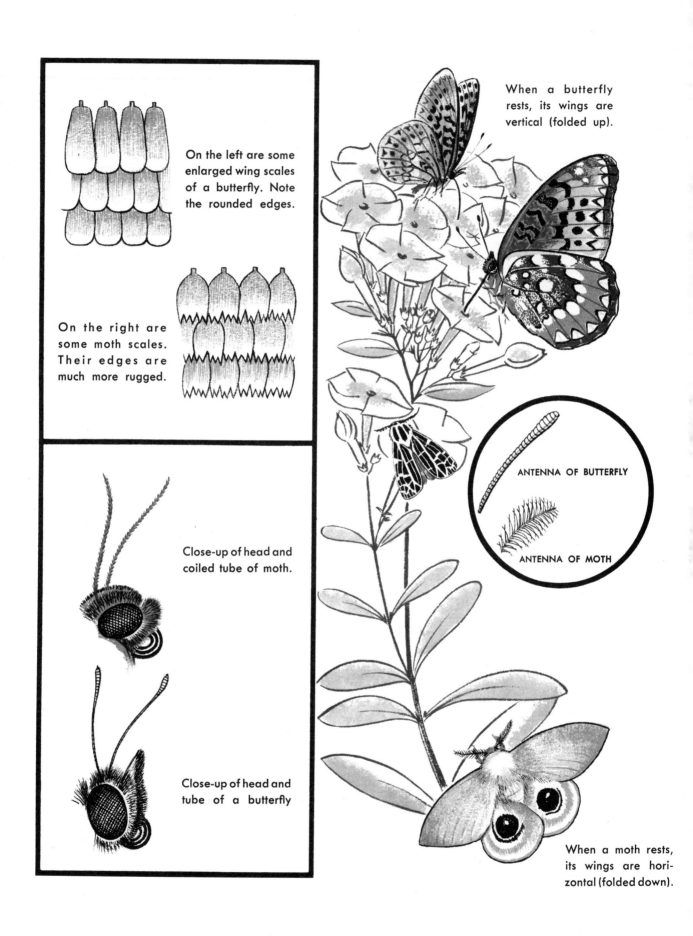

On the left are some enlarged wing scales of a butterfly. Note the rounded edges.

On the right are some moth scales. Their edges are much more rugged.

Close-up of head and coiled tube of moth.

Close-up of head and tube of a butterfly

When a butterfly rests, its wings are vertical (folded up).

ANTENNA OF BUTTERFLY

ANTENNA OF MOTH

When a moth rests, its wings are horizontal (folded down).

7. Ants, Bees and Wasps

If you see an insect with a slender waist,

How do ants, bees and wasps differ from other insects? the chances are that it is an ant, bee or wasp. If it has four clear-colored wings, you can be almost certain of it. Some flies and moths look like them, but flies have only two wings and moths have thick bodies.

Many of these insects live in large nests, so they are called "social insects." There is a queen that lays the eggs. She is cared for by the workers. They bring food and enlarge the nest for more new babies. All of the workers are females.

Sometimes the queen lays eggs which hatch into males. The males fly from the nest and mate with new queens. Then the queens start new nests of their own.

Not all bees live in hives. Carpenter

Where do bees live? bees dig holes in wood. Bumblebees make their home in holes in the ground. Sometimes they use an old mouse nest. They almost seem to be

QUEEN

WORKER

DRONE

A Honeybee Hive

The yellow cells are filled with pollen, the dark cells are ripe with honey, and the tan cells have young bees inside them.

paying the mice back for living in the hives of honeybees.

Mason bees lay their eggs in an old snail shell or knothole. A mason bee might even use a keyhole in a door for its home, cementing it shut with sand and clay.

Wasps and hornets were the first paper makers. Long

How does a wasp make its nest?

before humans learned to grind wood into paper, these insects were chewing bits of sticks, which they then

Paper wasps and their nest

mixed with saliva from their mouths. They shaped this material into nests. When it dried, they had a strong paper house in which to live.

Some wasps hunt and kill spiders. Others catch harmful caterpillars. Some of the smallest wasps thrust their eggs into the bodies of our garden pests. Then the tiny babies bore through the insect and kill it. They may be no larger than the size of the period at the end of this sentence.

How are wasps helpful to us?

Many ants are peaceful farmers or explorers. The terrible driver ants, however, eat everything in their path. Sometimes they enter jungle huts, and the natives flee for their lives. The driver ants chase away or kill every mouse and rat, insect and spider.

Why are some ants feared in the tropics?

Strange beetles, bugs and other insects live in the nests of many ants. They are usually not welcome, but they are not killed for some reason. When the ants are not looking, they steal some food, or even eat a few baby ants.

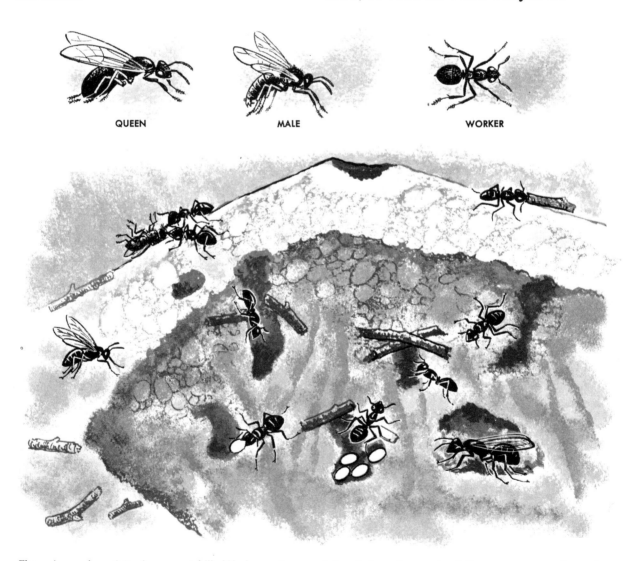

QUEEN   MALE   WORKER

There is much activity in an ant hill. Worker ants are pictured dragging a dead fly, a cocoon and a twig.

8. The Flies

When you catch a fly or mosquito, count

How is a fly different from all other insects?

its wings. The total may surprise you. All the other common insects have four wings, but the flies have only two. Instead of a second pair, they have a pair of knobs attached to the thorax. If these knobs are hurt, they cannot fly.

ANOPHELES MOSQUITO

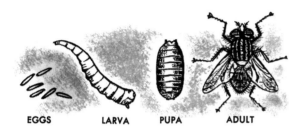

EGGS   LARVA   PUPA   ADULT

The life cycle of the housefly includes four stages.

One of the strangest flies lives in the fur

Do all flies have wings?

of some animals. It has no wings, and runs around in the hair of sheep, goats and deer. It looks like a big flea. A few other wingless flies live in the feathers of some birds. Still another, a wingless crane fly, can sometimes be seen walking around on the snow. It looks like a spider, but has only six legs instead of the spider's eight. It is one of the first insects to come out in the spring.

TSETSE FLY

A few tropical flies are among the most

Can flies be dangerous?

dangerous of all insects. The anopheles mosquito carries malaria disease from one person to an-

other. The aedes mosquito carries yellow fever. The tsetse flies of Africa carry sleeping sickness. Houseflies may go right from a garbage pail to your dinner table. Doctors worked many years before they found ways to control these insects. Many of them caught the same diseases they were fighting.

Some flies look like other insects. Some

How do some flies resemble other insects?

are colored exactly like a bee. Others look like wasps or hornets. Some look like moths. But if you count the wings, you'll see that they are not wasps and bees at all — they are flies.

BEE FLY

The bite of the black widow spider is

How can a fly kill a spider?

very poisonous. But one tiny fly has learned to go right into this spider's web without getting caught. It lays its eggs on the spider's egg sac, and the maggots burrow inside. They eat the eggs of the spider. Then they fly away. Without these little flies there would probably be many more black widow spiders, so this fly, at least, can kill a spider.

Insects and Plants

Many kinds of insects cause galls on plants. A gall is a swelling. Some are made by flies. The mother fly lays her eggs in the stem of a plant. The stem begins to swell. The eggs hatch inside the swelling. Then the maggots live in their strange house.

What causes plant galls?

A few plants feed on insects. They are called insectivorous plants. The pitcher plant has leaves which are hollow and shaped like a flower vase. Rain water falls into them and makes a little puddle. Insects fall into the water and drown. Then the plant digests the insects, somewhat as you digest the food you eat. Some pitcher plants are so large that they may trap frogs, lizards or even mice.

How do plants catch insects?

The sundew has sticky hairs on its leaves. Insects land on the leaves and get tangled in the sticky surface. Soon, like those in the pitcher plant, they are digested.

The milkweed catches insects, but it lets them go again. It has flowers with little traps in them. When an insect puts its foot in the trap, it is held fast. Then it struggles to get free. Finally the trap breaks off, and the insect flies away with it. Then when it visits another milkweed, grains of pollen in the trap fall out on the new blossom, so the milkweed can make its seeds.

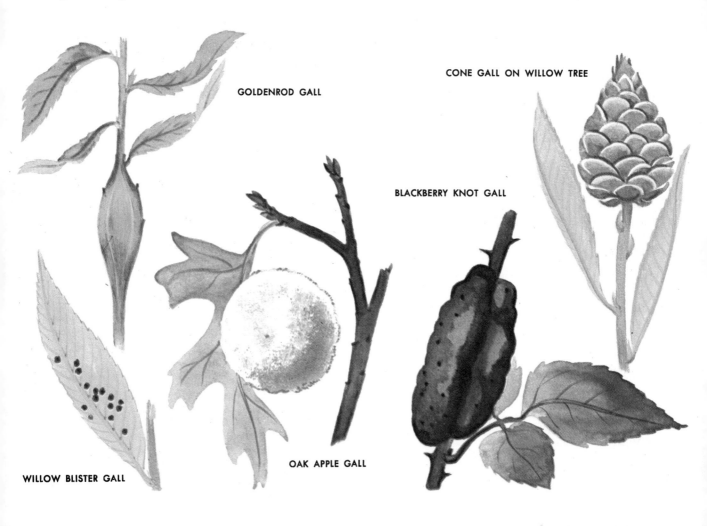

GOLDENROD GALL

CONE GALL ON WILLOW TREE

BLACKBERRY KNOT GALL

OAK APPLE GALL

WILLOW BLISTER GALL

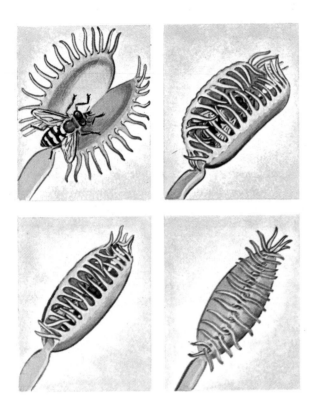

The Venus's-flytrap catches an insect.

An insect stuck in the hairs of a sundew plant

Some plants even live inside the bodies of insects. One fungus attacks houseflies and kills them.

What plants live inside of insects?

Another kind attacks caterpillars. Bacteria, which are so small that you need a microscope to see them, kill many others. Without these little plants, there would be even more insects in the world than there are now.

Many insects are useful in carrying seeds of plants. Small hooks on the seeds may catch in the hairs on the body of a fly or bee.

How do insects scatter seeds?

Then the seed is carried through the air as the insect flies away. Later it drops off and starts a new plant. Some insects take seeds to their nests in the ground. The seeds may grow, starting a new plant right in the middle of the nest.

One of the most interesting seeds is the Mexican jumping bean. This is a seed which contains a small caterpillar.

What is a Mexican jumping bean?

This little insect chews away at the inside of the seed. It changes position every few minutes. Every time it moves, the seed rolls around, just as you can roll a big box by moving around inside it. Finally the caterpillar turns into a little moth. Then it flies away to lay its eggs in new seeds.

41

Fossils and Prehistoric Insects

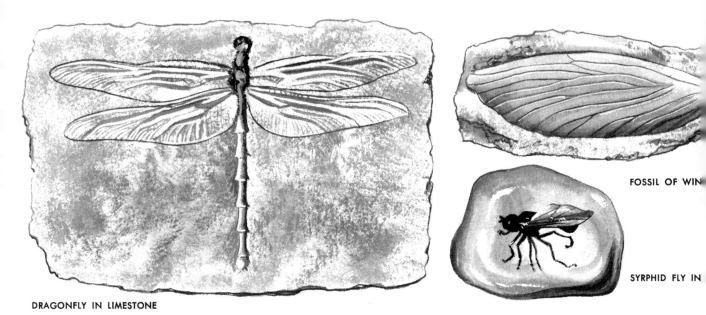

DRAGONFLY IN LIMESTONE

FOSSIL OF WIN

SYRPHID FLY IN

How are insect fossils made? If an insect, usually a large one, lands in soft mud or clay, it may get stuck there and eventually die. Frequently, the insect becomes completely buried in the mud, which may later turn into rock. When the insect wastes away, it leaves a natural print, or mold, of its body. Then, when the rock is broken, a picture-outline of the insect may be seen. Such prints and molds are known as "fossils."

What is an amber fossil? One of the most interesting insect fossils is the "amber fossil." Many kinds of trees, such as pines and spruces, have a sticky material known as resin. You may find it on the bark and trunk. Flies, ants, wasps and other insects often get tangled in this resin. More of it flows over them, covering them with a clear coating. Later this resin changes and hardens, becoming a substance known as amber. If there are insects inside, they will be preserved for millions of years by the hard material.

How old are some insect fossils? No one can be sure just when the first insects lived on this earth. Scientists have found insect fossils about 240 million years old. Some day they may find some that are still older. It is as interesting to hunt for fossil insects as it is to collect modern ones.

How large were prehistoric insects? If you could go backward about one million years, you would come to the days of the first cave man. Go back about 100 million years and you would see great dinosaurs. Go back still more, and you would see insect monsters. They would be even bigger than

42

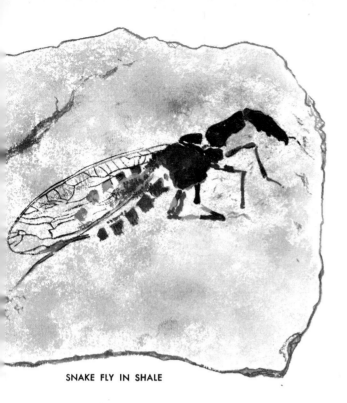

SNAKE FLY IN SHALE

Many of the smaller insects survived. Their descendants still crawl and fly around today. So you see that insects have been on earth a long time. Many scientists feel that they will still be here when all other animal life is gone.

Could there possibly be a giant insect somewhere the size of a human being? Scientists do not think so. Animals which are very large need some kind of blood system to carry oxygen to all parts of the body. Insects have blood, but it doesn't carry oxygen. The spiracles and air tubes are fine for a small insect, but they just wouldn't work for an insect the size of a man. Besides, a man-sized insect would not have any bones inside, any more than the small ones do. So it would have to have a heavy jacket of armor for strength. Such armor would make it too slow and clumsy.

Could insects get as large as people?

the Goliath beetle or the giant walking stick. Cockroaches as big as saucers would run over the ground. Insects which look like giant dragonflies would sail through the air like model airplanes. Their wings would be more than two feet across — almost seven times larger than many of our common dragonflies today!

The great insects lived at a time when much of the earth was warm and food was easy to find. The many plants grew so thickly that they formed great heaps of plant material. This was later compressed and hardened into coal. After the coal-forming period, the land grew cold and dry. Many insects died in the harsh climate. Perhaps they died from other causes, too. Scientists are still trying to find the reasons, like detectives solving a mystery millions of years old.

Why did the giant insects disappear?

The more we look at the world of insects, the more interesting it is. We can see tiger beetles with long hairs on their feet so they won't sink into the sand of the dunes where they live. We can watch "slug caterpillars" that seem to move along like a little bulldozer. Gold beetles look as if they were made of pure gold. Tumblebugs roll little balls of material along like children making a snowman. Water pennies look like coins crawling slowly along the bottom of a stream.

Collecting Insects

You can make an insect collection of
What do you need for an insect collection? your own, which is one of the best ways to get to know the insects. You will need these things:

(1) A magnifying glass.

(2) A pair of tweezers.

(3) A few dozen pins. (Regular insect pins are best. Perhaps a biology teacher can help you get some. If not, you may have to use common pins.)

(4) A box with a tight cover, such as a cigar box or a candy box.

(5) A piece of thick cardboard, cut to fit exactly into the bottom of the box. (With this, pins may be stuck in easily.)

(6) A killing jar. (This should have a tight lid. A pint-size jar will be fine. Put a crumpled piece of paper towel in the bottom, wet it with a few drops of cleaning fluid and force a circle of cardboard into the jar a little above the paper so that the insect cannot touch the damp paper. Keep the jar tightly closed when you are not using it.)

After you catch an insect, put it in the bottle for five minutes. It will quiet down right away. When it is still, take it out with the tweezers.

To keep your insect in good condition,
How should insects be mounted? carefully stick a pin through its thorax or chest from the top. Push the pin down until the pinhead is about one quarter of an inch above the insect's back. Beetles should have the pin stuck through the right wing. Put a small label on the pin, telling where and when you found the insect. If you know its name, put this on another label.

Stick the pin into the soft cardboard bottom of the box, and you'll be able to look at the insect whenever you wish. Always handle it with care after it is dry.

You can mount tiny insects, too. Glue them to one corner of a three-cornered piece of paper. Then push your pin through the center of the paper.

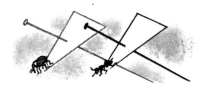

Butterflies and moths should have the
How should butterflies and moths be mounted? wings spread. Do this as soon as possible after collecting them. Don't let them dry out. Spread the wings flat on a piece of soft wood, one at a time, until all four wings are out straight. Hold them in place with strips

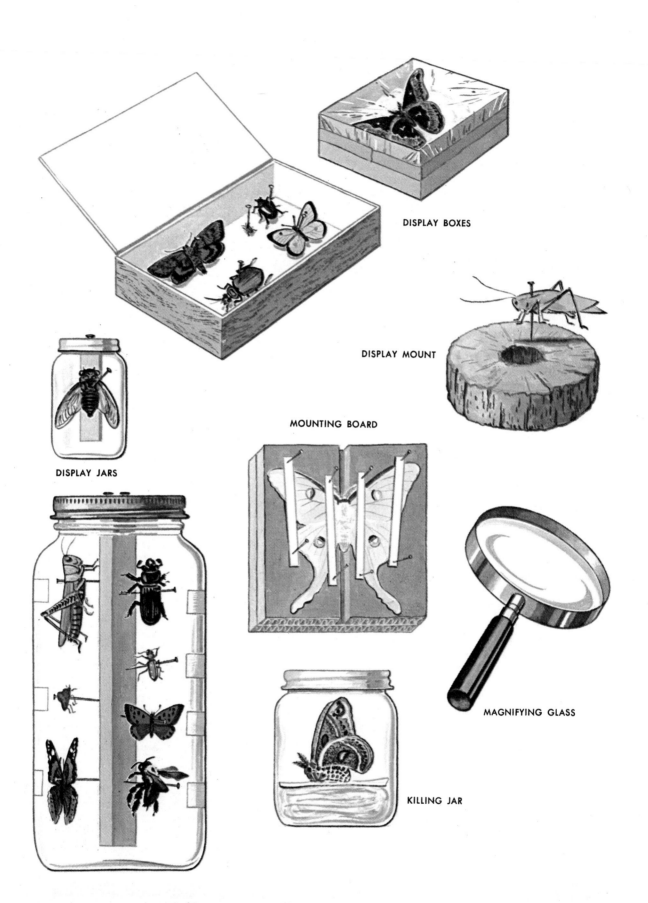

DISPLAY BOXES

DISPLAY MOUNT

DISPLAY JARS

MOUNTING BOARD

MAGNIFYING GLASS

KILLING JAR

of waxed paper. Never put pins through the wings.

If an insect gets hard and dry, it can be

How can dry insects be softened? relaxed and softened with steam from an iron. Place it in a saucer and let the steam from the iron point right at the insect. Or put it on a piece of wire screen over hot water. In a few minutes you can handle the insect without breaking it.

Put a few moth crystals in the box

How can your collection be protected from other insects? every three months. These are the same crystals used to protect winter clothing when it is stored away in the spring. Then other insects won't get in and eat up your collection. You can also keep insects in tiny bottles of alcohol. Regular rub-

bing alcohol is good. Their colors soon fade, but insects will stay soft.

You can make a little home for living

How can you make an insect home? insects. Then you can watch them grow and eat. Put some sand and twigs in a large glass jar. Put a small pill bottle filled with water in the sand. Then you can put leaves in the jar and the leaves will not dry up.

If you are raising a caterpillar, be sure you feed it plenty of the right kind of leaves. Use a good big jar, so that it will have plenty of room to spread its wings later.

You can make a little insect aquarium.

How can you keep water insects? Fill a goldfish bowl half full of water. Put in a few pebbles and weeds for hiding places. Keep it out of bright light or the

 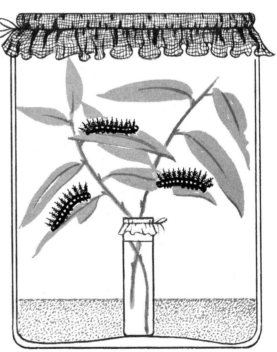

A jar with some water, a little sand and a covering made of plain gauze make a comfortable insect home.

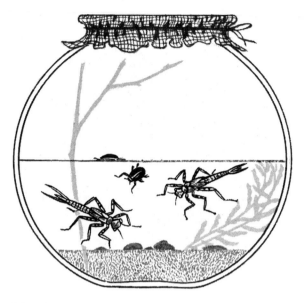

A bowl makes a comfortable home for water insects.

water will turn green. Then you can put any water insect in your aquarium. Cover the top, because most water insects can fly.

Your pets will feed on a bit of liver or fish. Serve it to them on a pair of tweezers, or hang it in the water by a thread. Take out, in an hour, all food that they don't eat. In that way, decaying food will not foul the water.

You can find insect eggs and cocoons

How can eggs and cocoons be kept from hatching too soon?

on twigs and dead leaves in winter. Keep them on the outside window sill until you are ready for them to hatch. The cold air will keep them fresh and healthy. If you keep them indoors where it is warm, they may hatch too soon.

A collector once brought in about a dozen praying mantis egg cases and left them on his desk. Then he forgot them.

In a few weeks there were hundreds of baby mantises all over the room.

You can make a fine display with your

How can you display your collection?

insect collection. Beetles, grasshoppers and dragonflies can be mounted in special boxes and then hung on the wall of your room. Mounted butterflies and moths make interesting "pictures" to hang on walls or to give as gifts.

To make a display case, find a large

How can you make a display case?

flat box, such as a writing paper box or candy box. Measure it and cut a piece of glass so that it will just fit over the box. Glue a picture hanger on the back of the box so it can be hung up later. Fill the box with cotton. It is a good idea to put some moth crystals in the cotton as protection against other insects.

Place your insects carefully on the cotton. Press them down so they will stay in place. Butterflies and moths should be mounted while they are still soft and flexible. Then put the glass plate over them and seal it neatly around the edges with tape. A coat of black enamel over the box and the tape will seal all the small holes and make a good-looking display case.

Some companies make black cases with white cotton just for insects. These are called Riker mounts. A biology teacher will be able to tell you where you can get them. The teacher can also tell you about special kits for mounting insects in a dish of liquid plastic. When

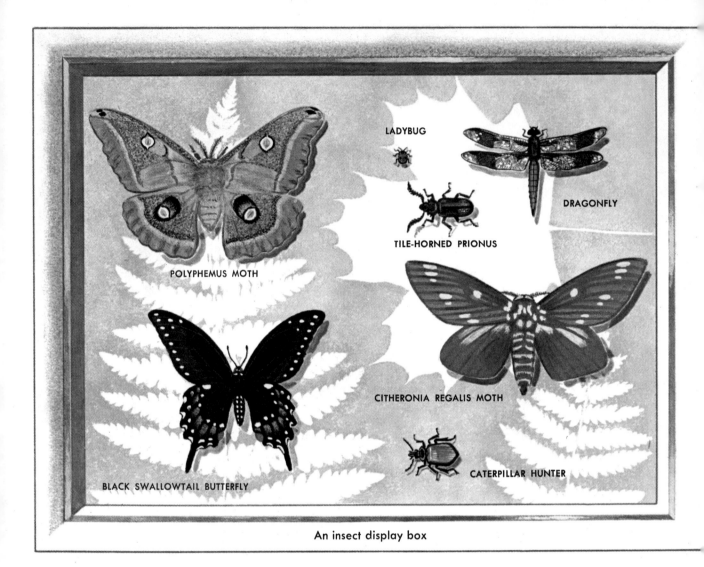

LADYBUG

DRAGONFLY

TILE-HORNED PRIONUS

POLYPHEMUS MOTH

CITHERONIA REGALIS MOTH

BLACK SWALLOWTAIL BUTTERFLY

CATERPILLAR HUNTER

An insect display box

the plastic hardens, you can take it out of the dish like an ice cube. Then it can be used as an ornament for your desk or as a gift.

A magnifying glass will help you learn

How can a magnifying glass help you?

much more about insects. It will show you many things too small to see without a lens. You may find an extra pair of eyes on the whirligig beetle, for instance. One is for seeing in the air, while the other is for looking under water. If you look in the center of a daisy, you'll see tiny black thrips. A close look at their legs shows that they walk around with feet that look like little balloons. Treehoppers look like prehistoric dinosaurs when they are seen under the magnifying glass.

In a few years, space ships may take men to Mars. They may even go beyond our own solar system. Some experts think they'll find strange new forms of life. But with a magnifying glass and a good sharp eye, we can stay home and find strange creatures of our own. Few animals that have ever lived are much stranger than the flies and beetles and bugs that live in the world right at our fingertips.

THE HOW AND WHY WONDER BOOK OF
ANTS AND BEES

Written by
RONALD N. ROOD

Illustrated by
CYNTHIA ILIFF KOEHLER
and ALVIN KOEHLER

Editorial Production:
DONALD D. WOLF

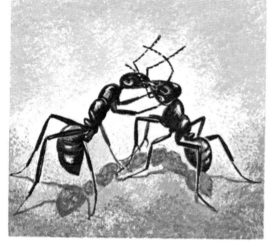

Edited under the supervision of
Dr. Paul E. Blackwood
Washington, D. C.

Text and illustrations approved by
Oakes A. White
Brooklyn Children's Museum
Brooklyn, New York

GROSSET & DUNLAP • **Publishers** • **NEW YORK**

Introduction

Anyone who doubts that truth is stranger than fiction need only study the habits of the social insects to have his opinion changed. For the life patterns of these six-legged animals reveal events of sheer wonder that could scarcely be imagined by the best fiction writer.

Scientists have studied the social insects for centuries, and a fairly complete picture of the peculiar and fascinating behavior of these insects is available. This *How and Why Wonder Book* accurately presents the essential characteristics of the four families of social insects — bees, wasps, ants and termites.

To a casual observer, many of the actions of social insects may appear strange. Are dancing bees really dancing? Are bumblebees being mischievous when they walk up to an intruder and plaster it with a gluey mess of honey? Whatever the appearance of such actions to a casual observer, close study shows that they are important to the insects in building and maintaining their insect society.

It is possible for anyone to watch social insects at close range. This can be done at home or in school by making an observation nest. Directions for making one are found in this book. Such a project is fun as well as instructive for individuals or class groups.

The study of social insects is a part of the science course in many schools. For this reason, *The How and Why Wonder Book of Ants and Bees* will be a useful addition to both home and school libraries.

Paul E. Blackwood

Dr. Blackwood is a professional employee in the U. S. Office of Education. This book was edited by him in his private capacity and no official support or endorsement by the Office of Education is intended or should be inferred.

Contents

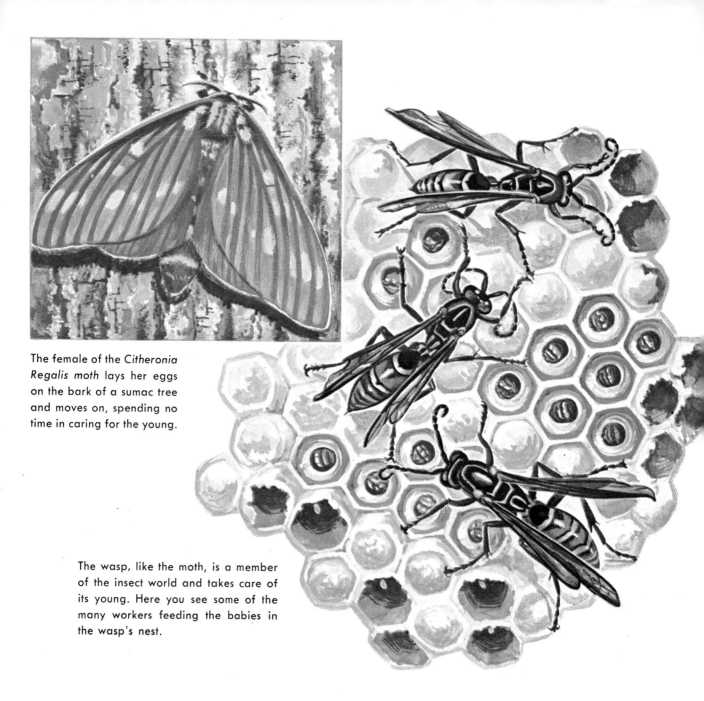

The female of the *Citheronia Regalis* moth lays her eggs on the bark of a sumac tree and moves on, spending no time in caring for the young.

The wasp, like the moth, is a member of the insect world and takes care of its young. Here you see some of the many workers feeding the babies in the wasp's nest.

SOCIAL INSECTS

The female moth creeps slowly along a tree limb. Finally she stops and lays a few eggs. They stick to the bark. Then she crawls away.

When her babies hatch, they must make their way by themselves. There are no parents to protect them. Alone, they must find food and hide from their enemies.

Most other insects do the same thing. The mosquito sets her eggs afloat on a little raft. Walking-stick insects just drop theirs on the ground. Other insects place their eggs where their young may find food and shelter. Then they leave them forever.

How strange it is, then, to see a wasp caring for her babies! She brings food, chews it up until it is soft and places it in their little mouths. She licks them, strokes them with her antennae, or "feelers," and builds a shelter to keep out the sun and the rain. If danger strikes, she flies toward it, even if it is an animal a thousand times her size.

Of all the insects, only bees, wasps, ants and termites take care of their families. The family, in turn, helps the mother to care for her later offspring. Because of this, and also because these insects live in little groups or societies, they are called "social insects."

Nobody is sure how the social habit developed. But scientists have noticed an interesting thing. Often, as soon as the young insects are given food, they produce little bubbles of saliva. The

Ants, like bees, are social insects. The fire ants above carry a larva and a cocoon to a safer place. Below are two termites licking each other. This is a process that, according to scientists, helps to keep the insect family together.

A bee will defend the hive against a larger enemy.

adult insects lick up the saliva quickly. Then the adults produce more saliva, which other adult insects lick up.

Does this special substance in the bubbles help to keep the insect family together? Many scientists think so. They call the process *trophallaxis* or "nursing together." As one scientist said, "To others in the nest, each insect must be a living lollipop."

What kinds of homes do these insects have in their hollow trees and paper nests? What happens after they have gone through the entrance hole and disappeared from sight? This book helps to tell their wonderful story.

BEES

(actual size)

The Castle of Wax

The honeybees come from every direction. Each one finds the target — an opening only an inch wide. Out of this opening stream other honeybees, circling for a moment before they dart away. The wax castle of the bees is humming with life.

Inside the opening is an amazing scene.

What is inside the wax castle? No factory ever ran with more bustle and activity. Hanging from the roof are heavy curtains of wax. They may be larger than this book and four times as thick. On both sides of the curtains are countless honeybees, poking their heads into hundreds of little cells or chambers.

This is the castle of ten thousand rooms.

How many rooms does it have? Each cell of the curtains is a little room by itself. Although we often speak of the curtains as "honeycomb," a great many of them do not contain honey at all. The cells of the brood comb each have a small inhabitant — a grublike larva that will soon turn into a new honeybee. For the larva, the cell is a cradle, living room and bedroom combined. The larva stays in it from the day it hatches until the day it is fully grown.

Nurse bees are walking all over the brood comb. Some-

What do the nurse bees do? times they put their feet right on the heads of the babies. One after the other, they bend down and poke their heads inside the cells. They feed and lick their little sisters in their cradles.

There is another kind of cell on the edge of the comb. It is much larger than the others. It looks almost like a peanut shell made out of wax. Inside it is a larva just like the thousands of others — only a little larger. This strange cell must be something special to be off on the side of the comb where it can have plenty of room. Indeed it is, for it is the royal nursery of the larva that will soon become the new queen.

Over on the true "honeycomb," some-

Why do bees evaporate their honey? thing strange is taking place. Bees are walking slowly over the half-filled cells, beating their wings as if they were trying to fly. As the breeze from their wings fans across the cells, it makes the sweet liquid evaporate. A cell that was filled with honey may be only three-quarters full the next day as a result of the air from their wings. This seems like a waste — to bring in nectar from the flowers and then evaporate it so there is not much left. But one taste of the liquid will tell why it is done. The sugar that stays behind as the water evaporates gets thicker and sweeter.

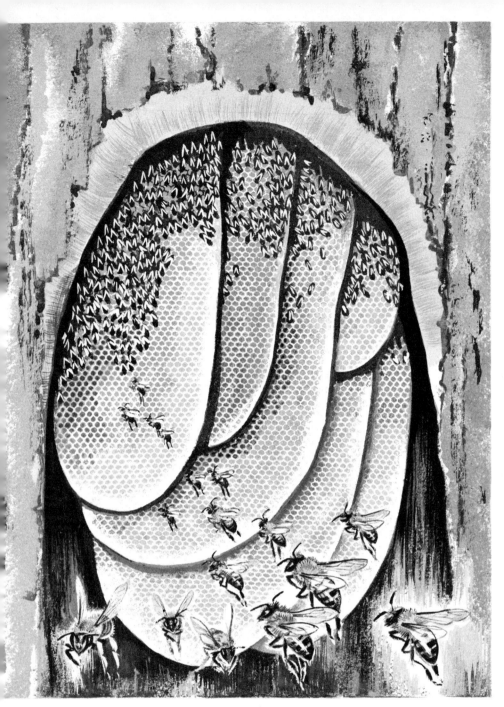

The wild beehive in a hollow tree clearly shows the various combs, hanging down like curtains and drapes in a home.

QUEEN

DRONE

WORKER

There are "pantry cells," too, for storage of pollen as food. But in another part of the hive is a comb that seems deserted. Each of the cells has been covered with a wax cap. They hang heavy and still, as if they have been forgotten. But they are filled with golden treasure — the nectar brought from the fields and changed in the bodies of the bees into thick, rich honey. Each pound of it is the work of many bees. Sometimes

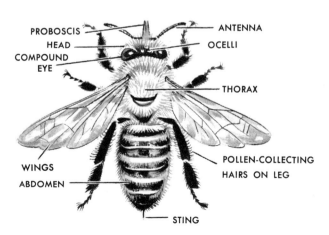

PROBOSCIS
HEAD
COMPOUND EYE
ANTENNA
OCELLI
THORAX
WINGS
ABDOMEN
POLLEN-COLLECTING HAIRS ON LEG
STING

The form, structure and vital parts of a bee (worker).

The building of queen cells gets special attention. They are larger than the other cells and are built at the edge of the comb so that they get more air. Some of the cells above are under construction. The one at the right is ready to receive an egg.

A living fan to condition air and condense honey.

work without being told. There are enough workers of each kind — nurses, honey-fanners, pollen-gatherers and wax-makers. If the hive gets too hot, some of the bees set up an air current with their wings as a ventilation system. If more wax is needed, extra bees set about making it.

Suddenly one bee appears that looks different from the others.

What is the job of the drone bee? Its head seems to be completely covered with two huge eyes, like a helmet. Its legs are shaped differently; its body is longer. It walks up to a worker bee and seems to ask for food. The worker stops work and gives it a bit of honey. Then it goes to another for more food, and so on. How strange to see this kind of bee in a bustling hive where all the others are working!

Yet this bee has a job, too. It is one of the most important of the bees. It is a drone, or male bee, one of a few dozen brothers among the thousands of worker sisters. Its job will begin when that peanut-shaped queen cell has opened and the new queen has made her

they have to make more than thirty-five thousand trips into the fields to produce a single pound of honey.

There may be thirty thousand bees in the hive, and each one has a job to do. There **How many bees live in a hive?** are no loafers. There are no supervisors to see that all are working. Every bee does its

If there is not enough food available, a worker might evict a drone from the hive.

The drone, unable to eat by itself, is fed by workers or it starves.

way into the world. For it must provide millions of tiny sperm cells that the queen bee stores in a special pouch in her body. Then, just before she places new eggs in the brood comb, she fertilizes each one with a sperm cell, so that it can develop into a new worker.

Once it was thought that the drones were lazy because they didn't help with the hive duties. But now we know that they couldn't help, no matter how much they wanted to. Their legs, heads and bodies are not shaped right for fashioning the wax into the perfect little chambers. They don't even have a sting with which they can help to drive away enemies. They just have those important little sperm cells, ready to be given to the queen in mating.

The "song of the hive" is a steady, high-pitched hum. It is made by the wings of the bees as they go about their work. Suddenly the song becomes louder. Then scratchings and squeaking can be heard. A mouse has tried to steal the honey. But the bees are always on their guard. They

What causes the "song of the hive"?

attack the mouse and drive it away from their nest.

Sometimes their attack is so fierce that they kill the mouse. Then they have a real problem. It's almost like having a dead elephant in the living room. If they don't do something quickly, the odor of the mouse will spoil the honey. But how can they get such a big creature out of the hive?

The answer lies in another kind of building material used by bees—*propolis* or "bee-glue." Quickly they get the sticky material from certain buds and twigs.

How do bees keep their hive clean?

9

Then they work it into a liquid which they use to cover the dead mouse. When it dries, it looks like tough brown paint. The mouse is sealed in its own little tomb, right inside the hive.

This is just one method of garbage disposal. The bees keep their hive clean at all times. Anything that doesn't belong there gets dumped outside. Sometimes a worker will drag out a protesting drone as if he were a piece of rubbish. Then the drone crawls back in again, and five minutes later the same worker may be giving him some honey.

No one is sure how the bees know what job they are supposed to do. But each one of them, doing its little task, helps the whole hive to operate like a big, humming machine. Sometimes the "machine" is located in a hollow tree. Other times it is in a specially-built beehive. The Bible tells us that Samson found bees in the body of a dead lion. But no matter where their home is located, the bees always build the same wax curtain-combs with the same six-sided cells, half an inch long and a quarter-inch wide.

The cells are so perfect and regular that the French scientist Réaumur once suggested they could be used as a unit of measurement.

How can the honeybee do all her many jobs and make such perfect wax cells? Some of the answers will be found in the next chapter.

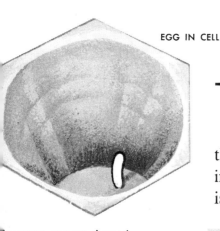

EGG IN CELL

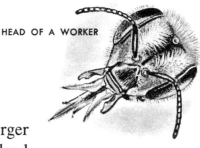

HEAD OF A WORKER

The Magic of Bees

From a blind, helpless baby no larger than a grain of sugar to a full-fledged insect with a whole set of tools — that is the story of the honeybee. It begins

The gray, comma-shaped egg is attached to the bottom of the cell with an adhesive secretion.

A blind and legless grub hatches from the egg. It is fed continuously until it starts spinning a cocoon after a few days.

WORKER FEEDING LARVA

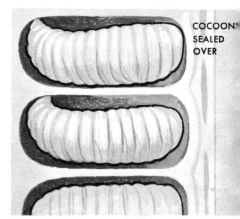

COCOON SEALED OVER

life as a tiny comma-shaped egg. It can hardly be seen in the cell that seems so huge in comparison. It hatches three days after it is placed there by the queen mother. But it doesn't look like a bee at all. It is just a white, legless, blind grub that seems to be all appetite.

Food is near at hand. A few minutes after the grub has hatched, the head of a full-grown bee appears at the grub's cell. Poking down to the new arrival, the adult bee supplies it with "royal jelly" — a paste made in special glands in the bee's head. No sooner has it fed the little larva and gone on to the next cell than another load of food arrives. Then another comes, and another, and another — about once every minute.

How does a new bee get its food?

Instead of choking on all this food, the larva begins to swell like a balloon. Its skin gets tighter, like a jacket that is too small. Soon it splits and the grub wriggles free. The next day it molts, or sheds its jacket, again. Finally, the larva has become so large that it fills its cell. It has been fed about ten thousand times — royal jelly

How does the baby bee grow?

for the first two days and "bee bread," or flower pollen mixed with honey, for four more. Now it is as big as the eraser on the end of a new pencil—more than a thousand times larger than it was a week ago.

It begins to produce a sticky silk from glands near its mouth. Weaving back and forth, it spins the silk into a lacy cocoon. Then it lies still, like a mummy wrapped in cloth.

All over the brood comb, hundreds of other bee larvae are doing the same thing. The queen mother that laid the eggs may have produced a thousand that same day — placing each in its own six-sided cell. Just before the larvae start to form cocoons, the nurse bees seal their rooms with wax. Then they go on to the care of other babies.

Inside the cocoon there is a great change. The soft, legless grub body stiffens. Outlines of legs, wings, eyes, antennae, or "feelers," begin to form. The larva is a larva no longer, but a pupa — darkening, hardening, full of promise of the honeybee to come.

Twelve days later, a sharp new pair of jaws begins to cut away at the wax cap of the cell. Now comes the greatest marvel of all. The cell opens and out comes a clean new honeybee — her

WORKERS (ACTUAL SIZ

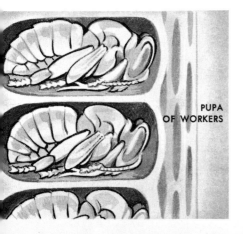

PUPA OF WORKERS

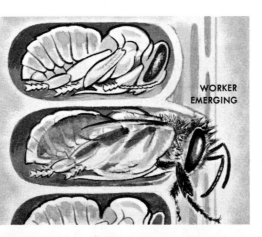

WORKER EMERGING

Here, in the cocoon, the great change takes place: from grub to milk-white nymph or pupa, until one day the adult bee emerges. If the egg is fertilized, the bee will become a worker. If not fertilized, it will become a drone.

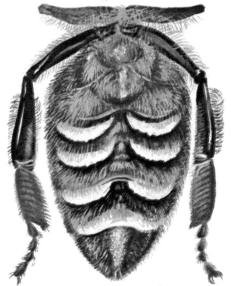

The wax can be seen in this close-up view of the underside of a worker bee.

To make wax for building new cells, bees hang in chains from combs. Thin slips of wax come from their abdominal plates as they stretch themselves.

four shining wings thinner than paper, her six legs ready to cling to the petals of the flowers she has never seen. Scientists say that such a change, from a grub to a bee, is as wonderful as putting a truck into a garage, closing the door and taking out a beautiful new airplane twelve days later.

All around her are hundreds of other workers, busy at their tasks. After buzzing her new wings and stretching her new legs for a day or so, she goes to work herself. She feeds pollen and honey to her younger sisters, all ready to build cocoons of

What does a new worker do?

their own. Then in a few days, the glands in her head begin to make royal jelly for the newborn babies. One of them may be growing in the same cell she occupied just a few days before.

New wax is needed for the comb. The young worker takes great drinks of honey and then "hangs herself up" in a sheet of living bodies with her sisters. Each one hangs with her front feet attached to the hind legs of the one above. After a few hours little plates of wax appear on each abdomen. Wax oozes out through special glands. Shaping the wax with the jaws and feet,

How is beeswax made?

12

the bees build new cells like the thousands already there.

A bee cannot always produce beeswax. Nor can it always produce royal jelly. The life of bees runs in a series of stages. Once the bee has passed a certain point, it does not go back again. Young workers can make royal jelly for a few days. Then they can make wax. Then, when they are older, they go out into the fields to gather nectar and pollen. So if we know what kind of work a bee is doing, we have some idea of how old it is.

When she leaves the hive, the worker is almost like a puppy in a strange new yard. She flies around and around, never straying far from the hive. Her great compound eyes take in the form of rocks and trees nearby. The six thousand "smell-plates" on her antennae receive strange odors from the new world, but she doesn't venture away

until a day or two later. Then she begins the job that will last the rest of her life.

She carries her tool kit right with her.

What is the bee's tool kit? It is in the form of bristles and spines on her legs. She has a pair of "pollen baskets" on her hind legs to stuff full of the golden powder from flowers. Her front legs have cleaning brushes for the delicate antennae. Spines on the middle legs help pry pollen out of the pollen baskets. Other spines help her trim and shape the wax for the comb.

When she goes from one flower to another, she pokes her head deep into its center to get the sweet nectar. Hairs on her body brush the powdery pollen around. She stuffs it in her pollen baskets. Then some of it rubs off as she brushes around in the next flower.

The bees collect pollen on their hind legs. Pollen is held in place by long leg hairs, which form the so-called "pollen baskets" (right).

With its long proboscis, the bee sucks the nectar that is produced in the bottom of the flower. In doing so, the bee pollinates the flower, making it possible to produce seeds (below).

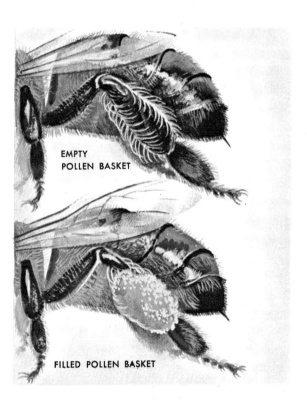

EMPTY POLLEN BASKET

FILLED POLLEN BASKET

The more circles a bee "dances," the farther away are flowers with nectar.

Why do farmers like the bees? Mixed from flower to flower, pollen is needed for blossoms to develop their fruit and seeds. The seeds can grow into new plants. If the bees didn't scatter the pollen, there would probably be no orchards. Apples, peaches, strawberries, oranges and other fruit would be unknown. There would be no pretty flowers in the garden. The honey produced by bees in the United States alone is worth about a hundred million dollars each year. This, however, is small compared to the value of all the fruit and flowers.

Why doesn't the pollen from a dandelion get mixed with the flower from a rose? Simply because the honeybee visits only one kind of flower at a time. She may fly over a whole field of dandelions to get to a rose garden. The next day, she may visit nothing but clover.

An apple tree begins to unfold its flowers early one May morning. By eight o'clock, hundreds of fragrant pink-and-white blooms have opened. A single bee discovers them. She takes nectar from a few blossoms. Then she stuffs her baskets with pollen, circles around for a few seconds and is gone. In less than half an hour the tree is buzzing with dozens of honeybees. How did she tell them about her wonderful find of a tree full of flowers?

What are the "dancing bees"? The answer was found by Dr. Karl von Frisch of Germany, when he discovered the "dancing bees." When the worker returned from the apple tree, she began to do a little dance near the entrance to the hive. First she circled one way, then another. In between the circles she walked a little straight line, wiggling like an excited puppy. Soon the others followed her in her dance, doing just the same as she was doing. The circles tell how far away the flowers are — the more circles, the farther away. The straight line tells the direction to travel, and the odor of the flowers still clinging to her body tells them what kind of flowers they will find. In a few minutes they fly away, one after another — right to the apple tree!

How is honey made? Every worker is a little chemistry laboratory. When she stuffs herself full of nectar, she stores it in a little pouch in her abdomen, the "honey stomach." There it is changed in a process

14

The straight line in the bee's dance shows the direction of the flower. The tail-wagging gives the scent.

sends it down. Ultraviolet light, too — the same invisible rays that cause a sunburn — guides the bees. And their huge compound eyes make out the shape of familiar trees and houses. They find their way by the colors of flowers, too — all but one color. The bees are color-blind to red.

that is still a mystery. Somehow it becomes thin honey, which is like nothing else on earth. Man has tried for years to learn to make honey out of sweetened water or even the nectar of flowers. But so far he has been defeated. Whether honey is in a honeycomb, in jars on a supermarket shelf, in cough syrup or spread on a slice of bread, every drop of it has been made by honeybees.

How do bees find their way?

Beekeepers know that bees find their way by means of the sun. But what do they do on a cloudy day? They can still sense where the sun is in the sky by means of polarized light. This is light that can be seen better from one direction than from others. Even behind the clouds, the sun still

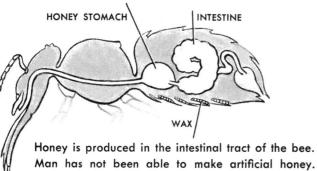

HONEY STOMACH | INTESTINE

WAX

Honey is produced in the intestinal tract of the bee. Man has not been able to make artificial honey.

How long do bees live?

Day after day the bee travels back and forth. Little hooks between her wings hold them together for strength in flight. The wings buzz as much as two hundred times per second. But in a few days they begin to get frayed on the edges. In a couple of weeks they are slightly torn. A little more than a month from the time she first spread their shining beauty in the sun, the faithful wings are tattered.

She works with them until she can fly no longer. One day she finds her load of pollen and nectar too heavy. The bee drops to the ground, half-crawling, half-flying toward the hive. There, six or eight weeks after she visited her first flower, her days of work come to an end.

Why does a bee die when it stings?

She may give her life in another way, too. If an enemy strikes, she flies to the attack. She drives her sting deep into its flesh. But as she pulls away the little barbs on the sting hold fast. It is pulled out of her body, leaving her torn and dying. Although a bee sting means pain for the victim, it means death for the honeybee.

No matter what happens to the workers, life in the hive goes on. The new babies receive their two days of royal jelly followed by pollen and honey. But the larva in the queen cell continues to get royal jelly every day. This makes a wonderful change. Instead of a regular-sized worker, unable to lay eggs, the diet of royal jelly will produce a sleek new queen.

Even though the queen has not yet left her cocoon, a strange sound is coming from her cell. It can be heard above the song of the hive.

A new princess is about to be born.

A queen honeybee emerges from the irregular wax cell in which she has developed.

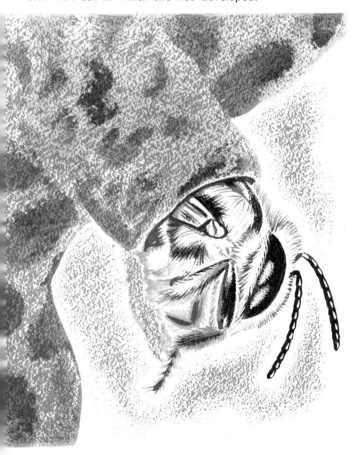

The Captive Queen

The new queen is one third larger than

What does the new queen look like?

the workers. Her legs lack their tools and combs. Her wings are folded and damp against her body, but they are vibrating with a high-pitched hum that pierces the walls of the hive. Quickly she bites at the top of her cocoon and the cap of her queen cell.

At last she is free. Scarcely waiting for her wings to dry, she rushes over the brood comb. The workers make way for her. Finally, she finds what she is seeking. Another queen cell is waiting. From it, too, comes the strange song. The workers stand by as she tears at the cap until she has opened it. Then she thrusts her sting deep, again and again. Unlike the workers, she can use her long, curved sting many times. But she uses it only against other queens.

If two queens emerge from cocoons at the same instant, there is a duel. The insects thrust at each other with their sharp stings until only one of the queens is left alive.

She can no more stop from stinging her

Why does she kill her sister queens?

sister queens than the workers can stop gathering in the fields. "One queen per hive" is the rule that she must follow. She may have six or eight other queens seeking to destroy her if she allows them to live. Only after she has made sure that she is the only queen bee in the hive does she finally stop to rest.

QUEEN BEE
(ACTUAL SIZE)

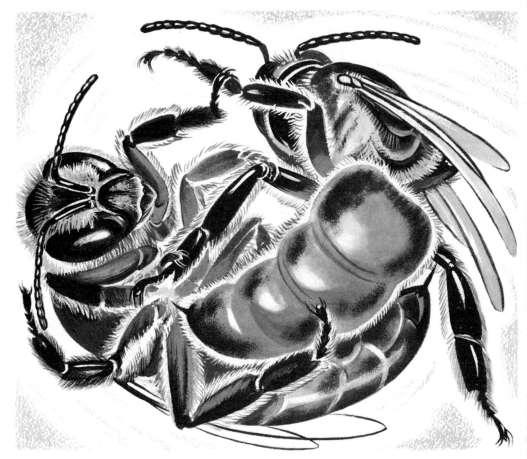

"One queen per hive" is the rule she must follow. If two queens emerge from their cocoons at the same instant, a battle to the death develops. Here two queens duel it out.

If there is only a single queen for each hive, what will happen when she meets her queen mother? To find the answer we have to go back a few days. The queen mother put a normal egg into each special cell as she came to it. Fed only royal jelly by the workers, each one developed into a queen larva. Then, as the time came near for their emergence as new queens, a change came over the entire hive.

What happens to the old queen mother?

Gone is the old need to spend every moment working in the fields. Even the queen mother's constant job of laying eggs is forgotten. Tearing open the caps of the honeycomb, thousands of bees drink so deeply that they become stuffed. This is probably a wise provision by nature for the time ahead. For this is known as the time of the swarm.

The queen mother and several thousand of her family will leave the hive forever to find a new home.

The workers are so full that some of them can hardly fly. Many, like the fat man who couldn't bend over to tie his own shoe, are unable to curve their abdomens enough to use their stings. In fact, they seem too good-natured to sting. The song of the hive rises to a new pitch. Everything is in preparation for a great adventure.

Finally the great day comes. The sun is shining and the weather is fair—the beekeepers call it a "swarm day." The bees fly out by the hundreds and thousands. Away they go to a nearby tree or bush where they cluster in a close mass. The ones on the outside of the mass open little scent-

What is a "swarm day"?

17

hollow tree or empty hive. The swarm follows them to the new home.

Sometimes the beekeeper wishes to find the queen. Then he may shake the swarm into a tub of water. As the bees begin to swim toward the sides, he can usually find her by her large size. Occasionally, he discovers that the bees have swarmed without her. This is like having a birthday party for someone who didn't get invited. The swarm cannot live more than a few days without its queen. Only she can lay the eggs to produce new workers.

The queen, whether it is the new queen back in the hive, or the queen mother in the swarm, is not really a ruler. She is more like a prisoner than a queen. She must be fed and cared for by her workers. Except for her swarming and mating flights, she never sees the outside world.

How is the queen like a prisoner?

The old queen has left. Now the new queen pushes toward the opening of the

Bees are easily irritated, but they will often allow themselves to be handled this way on swarm days.

glands on their abdomen and fan the scent out into the air with their wings. They do this to guide others to the spot, just as they often do when they find a rich source of nectar or a cluster of flowers.

The clustered swarm is thick and heavy. It can often be shaken from the bush into an empty hive like a huge bunch of overripe grapes. Somewhere in the center of the swarm is the queen mother. Soon some bees have found a

hive. A most important job waits for her. At last the drones will get a chance to do their part. She takes off on her new wings, circling around and around. The drones follow. Sometimes she goes out of sight.

Finally she mates with one of the drones. She may **What happens to the drones after mating?** choose one from another hive as far as nine miles away. The millions of tiny sperm cells from the drone's body are placed in a pouch in the queen's abdomen. His work done at last, the drone soon dies. The other drones are driven from the hive when the food supply gets low in the fall.

Back in the hive, she becomes the new queen mother. Day **How many eggs does the new queen produce?** after day she lays thousands of eggs —often four or five thousand a day. Such egg production is a great task. So she is fed by the workers almost constantly. They feed her and lick her, caring for her every need.

Perhaps this licking and passing around material from her **What happens if the queen is taken away?** body serves to keep the hive going smoothly. If the queen is taken away or dies, the workers create a new queen by enlarging a cell and keeping one of the newborn babies on a steady royal jelly diet. If this doesn't work, the workers themselves manage to lay a few eggs, but these develop only into drones. Then the hive, without a queen, soon dies.

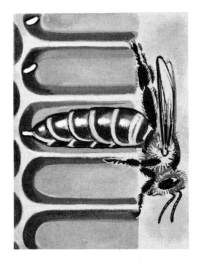

A queen laying eggs.

If nothing happens to the queen, she may live with her **How long does the queen live?** huge family for four or five years. During this time she may lay a million eggs. What a difference between the queen mother and the single moth who leaves a few eggs on a twig in the fall!

But there are many other bees, too. They live in interesting places — old mouse nests, hollow chunks of wood, even tin cans. Their story will be told in the next chapter.

Attendants constantly surround the queen. When she pauses in her egg-laying, they clean and feed her.

Bees Without a Hive

A bee that doesn't sting! It is hard to believe, but there are bees in South America that never sting at all. They live in colonies, or large families, just like the honeybees. Instead of living in a man-made hive, they make their homes in hollow trees or caves. Here they build combs out of wax and clay or from the sticky resin of trees.

Since they don't sting, they have a different way of protecting their little honeypots and the larvae in the cells. When an enemy comes, they fly all over it, biting and scratching. Strong fluid from their mouths and bodies causes a burning sensation. It feels almost like spattering grease. But even so, South American natives often keep them in little "drums." These are made of a hollow log with both ends sealed, except

How do stingless bees fight enemies?

for a little hole for the bees to enter. When the natives want some honey, they just break open the end of a drum.

Often this honey is delicious. But sometimes it is not. The stingless bees visit all kinds of flowers. If there aren't enough flowers available, they take the next best thing. This may be a molasses can or an old grapefruit peel, with a drop or two of motor oil for variety. A South American meal with native honey must be full of surprises!

The honeybee and the stingless bees take care of the eggs laid by the queen. But many of the other kinds of queens take care of their own eggs. One of the strangest is the queen bumblebee. She sits on her eggs in the spring

How is a queen bumblebee like a mother bird?

An apiary (a place where bees are kept) set in a landscape with fruit trees is always an interesting sight. The large "boxes" are actually modern beehives. They have replaced the less practical straw skeps (inset at right) that were used for a long time throughout the whole world. The movable frames of the modern hive (cross section on page 20) is much more convenient for the beekeeper and for the bees as well. The queen and the young can get only to section "B," leaving the honey in the top combs undisturbed for the keeper.

spring flowers. The other is her brood cell. About eight eggs go into it, often on a little pad of pollen that will serve as food. Then she caps it over with wax and settles down on top of it.

For the queen bumblebee, babysitting is no problem. When the larvae hatch in three or four days, she opens their cell to feed them. But when they are fed, she closes it up again. She may do this several times a day, flying away for more food in between.

like a little bird. All winter long she remains in a sheltered spot, hidden from the cold and storm. When spring comes at last, she goes house-hunting. She flies over the meadow, looking for a little hollow in the ground. Sometimes she even uses an old mouse nest or a half-hidden tin can.

She makes two wax cells. One of them is her honeypot. She fills it with honey she has made from the early

Close-up of the head of a stingless bee and the log shed in which Mexican Indians of Yucatán keep them.

LARVAE IN SHELLS

COCOONS

Only the bumblebee, which can reach the nectar, is able to pollinate red clover.

What are the bumblebee's enemies? When she leaves home, she may get into all kinds of trouble. Some kinds of birds like to eat bumblebees — sting and all. A huge robber fly, looking like a bumblebee itself, may lie waiting in a flower, ready to catch her. Sometimes she comes across the nest of another bumblebee. In she goes, just as if it were her own home. She may even drive out the rightful queen and settle down on the eggs herself. This is hard on the babies back at her own home. Sometimes the homeless queen finds the unoccupied nest and begins to take care of it. Thus the two "mothers" have switched nests. More often, an unprotected nest is found by a mouse that helps itself to the tender baby bees and honey.

What are "callows"? The queen helps the new workers, called "callows," out of their cells. Now they are about three weeks old. They are wet and silver-looking at first — hardly like the fuzzy black and yellow queen. Creeping to the honeypot, they help themselves. In a day or two, they are flying over the fields. Sometimes they are caught in a shower, but they just go inside a hanging flower. It shelters them like a sweet-scented umbrella.

Bumblebees seldom sting. They are peaceful, hard-working creatures, but they can sting again and again when necessary. They attack by clawing, biting and scratching. Although there may be only a few hundred bumblebees in a colony, with only fifteen or twenty at home at a time, few creatures make an effort to steal the honey from the little waxen pots.

How is honey used by bees for defense? Strange as it seems, even the honey is used for defense by some kinds of bumblebees. If an enemy attacks, a bumblebee quietly walks up to it, a drop of honey on its tongue. Then the bee plasters the intruder with the gluey stuff. Messy and dripping, the enemy retreats as fast as its sticky feet will let it.

22

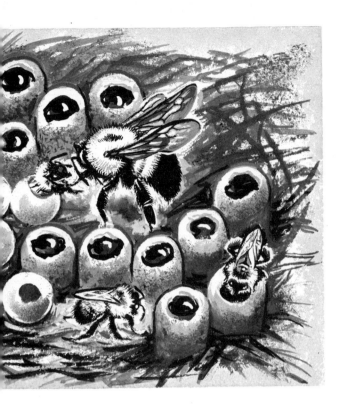

care for themselves. Finally, when they are ready to emerge, each one bites through the hard walls of its home and comes into the world.

Sometimes African explorers come across the ruins of an ancient city. The walls are covered with the hard plaster of the mason bees. The explorers chip away at it, scraping carefully. Sometimes, after they have removed it, they come to nothing but a blank wall. Other times, they come to ancient writings or stone-pictures. These important findings have been hidden for many centuries by the work of these little cement-makers, the mason bees.

There are about ten thousand kinds of

How many kinds of bees are known? bees known in the world today. Only a few of them are social kinds living in families. There are "cuckoo" bees that sneak into nests of other bees and lay their eggs. Others steal honey to feed their own young. Burrowing bees make holes in the ground. Sweat bees cling to men and animals in summer, lapping the sweat from their bodies. Leafcutting bees trim slices of leaves that they paste together for their homes.

To tell the stories of all the bees would take many books. But there are many more kinds of social insects. The next chapter will tell about the wonderful world of wasps, regarded as among the most intelligent of insects.

The jaws of the carpenter bee are strong

What is a carpenter bee? little tools. The bee itself looks like a bumblebee, but makes its home in wood. Hollowing out a tunnel in a beam or board with its jaws, it builds a little chamber for its eggs. Sometimes these tunnels may twist and turn through lumber for eight or ten feet. Some carpenter bees save themselves a lot of work. They build their nests in hollow bamboo stems. Thus the tunnel is already made for them to live in.

The jaws of mason bees bite through

How do mason bees build their homes? sand and clay. The mother builds her nest out of mud and fills it with pollen and nectar. The mud hardens until it is like stone. The larvae inside feed and

LEAFCUTTER NEST   LEAFCUTTING BEE

CARPENTER BEE

MASON BEE

BURROWING BEE

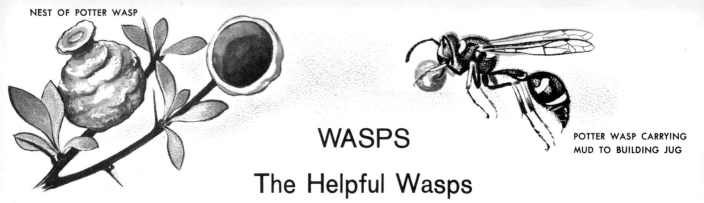

POTTER WASP CARRYING
MUD TO BUILDING JUG

WASPS

The Helpful Wasps

Nearly everybody likes fig bars. There

What is a fig wasp?

wouldn't be a single one if it weren't for the tiny fig wasp. She wanders around on the blossom of the fig, spreading the pollen and making it possible for the fruit to develop. Her young hatch out and seek new blossoms. This valuable insect was actually imported into California for the production of Smyrna figs.

There are about ten thousand kinds of

How many kinds of wasps are there?

wasps. Only a few of them are social.

Most of them live their lives quietly and unseen. Some of their relatives, the horntails and sawflies, attack trees and fruit, but a great many of the true wasps are as useful as honeybees.

The tomato hornworm caterpillar is a

How do wasps help farmers?

bad garden pest. It feeds on the leaves of tomato vines and

damages the blossoms. A tiny wasp, the

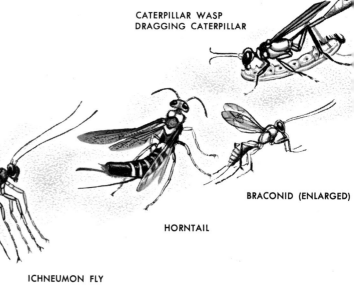

CATERPILLAR WASP
DRAGGING CATERPILLAR

BRACONID (ENLARGED)

HORNTAIL

ICHNEUMON FLY

braconid, pokes her sharp abdomen into the caterpillar several times. Each thrust may release a dozen eggs. The young feed on the pest, finally coming outside to make their little cocoons. The caterpillar soon dies.

Other braconid wasps can produce a whole family with just one egg. This is done when a certain wasp finds the

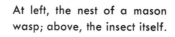

At left, the nest of a mason wasp; above, the insect itself.

caterpillar of harmful fruit moths or corn borers. Although she is tiny, her amazing egg makes up for her lack of size. After she lays it, it begins to divide into many little cell-groups. Each group produces a hungry larva. It feeds on the body of the caterpillar. Then just as the caterpillar dies, the newborn wasps fly away.

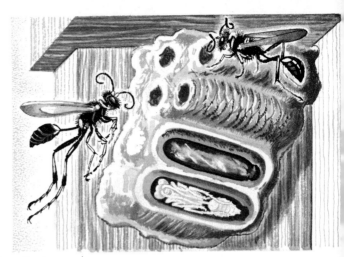

A mud-dauber nest and wasps and two opened cells.

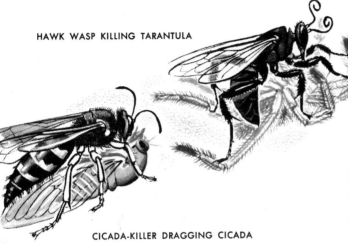

HAWK WASP KILLING TARANTULA

CICADA-KILLER DRAGGING CICADA

A single egg may produce fifty or more wasps. Then if each wasp produces fifty more, there will be twenty-five hundred wasps in a few weeks, all looking for fruit moths.

A huge ichneumon wasp goes flying through the air. It stops at a dying maple tree. Slowly it crawls over the bark, tapping with its antennae. Finally it stops and arches its back. A long thread-like organ, the *ovipositor,* goes to work. Sharp-pointed and strong, it drills deep into the wood.

Why do some wasps drill into trees?

Often people kill this wasp when they see it drilling into a tree. But this is just what shouldn't be done. For the wasp drills until she comes to the tunnel of a wood borer, the real villain. The wasp's larva, hatching out, will destroy the wood borer before it can kill any more trees.

Some wasps are even hitchhikers. One, known as Phanurus, rides around on a moth like a man on a horse. Then, when the moth finally lays its eggs, the little hitchhiker gets off. She lays her own eggs on the moth eggs. Both may start to develop, but it is only the little wasps that hatch out and fly away.

What wasp is a hitchhiker?

The Bible tells of plagues of locusts, which still bother people in many parts of the world. When the female locust lays her eggs underground, the Scelio wasp waits nearby. As fast as the locust buries new eggs, the wasp pokes her ovipositor down into them and lays eggs of her own. The two may work side by side — the locust laying eggs and the wasp destroying them.

25

Hunter wasps catch and paralyze spiders with a care-

How do hunter wasps feed their young? fully-placed sting. Sand wasps do the same with caterpillars. The spider or caterpillar is then placed in the cell of the wasp's nest. Three or four more victims may be added. Then the wasp lays an egg. The new larva has fresh food until it becomes fully grown.

Mud-dauber wasps make many of their homes out of mud, almost like the mason bees. Often they can be seen against the sides of buildings or under roofs. Filled with paralyzed spiders, each cell of the home soon opens to release a new wasp. Potter wasps make little mud jugs and stock them with caterpillars.

How do the wasps catch the spiders? Often a wasp may hang by one leg from the web and sting the spider when it rushes out to catch it. The "tarantula hawk" wasp stings the huge, hairy tarantula and then buries this spider with the wasp egg.

Strange growths appear on the leaves and stems of plants.

What do gall wasps do? They may look like brown apples, little porcupines, bits of moss. Many of these are made by gall wasps. The female pokes her eggs into the plant, which then forms the gall. Just how it forms is not fully understood. The larvae feed on the material inside the home that the plant has helpfully made. Often they spend the entire winter in this shelter. Each kind of insect produces a definite kind of plant gall.

None of the wasps in this chapter are true social insects. But a few wasps live in families, like their cousins the bees. Most of them make their homes in paper nests.

The next chapter will describe what takes place inside the walls of these paper palaces.

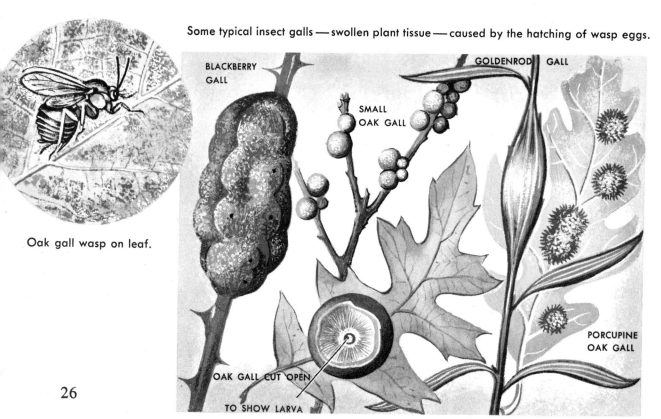

Some typical insect galls — swollen plant tissue — caused by the hatching of wasp eggs.

Oak gall wasp on leaf.

BLACKBERRY GALL

GOLDENROD GALL

SMALL OAK GALL

OAK GALL CUT OPEN TO SHOW LARVA

PORCUPINE OAK GALL

HEAD OF POLISTES WASP
(ENLARGED)

The Paper Palace

HEAD OF BALD-FACED HORNET
(ENLARGED)

How long ago was the first paper made?

When was paper originally made? Was it over five hundred years ago, when Johann Gutenberg printed a Bible in 1455? Two thousand years ago, when the Chinese made paper from mulberry bark? Four thousand years ago, when the Egyptians wrote on flat sheets from the papyrus reed? The truth is that paper was first made *millions* of years ago. No human hand touched that first sheet of paper. It was probably manufactured in much the same way as it is today — by a queen wasp, making a shelter for her eggs and larvae.

She goes to a piece of dried wood on a

How do wasps make paper? tree or the side of a house. Her strong little jaws work like scissors. She cuts chunks of wood and mixes them with her saliva. Getting all she can carry, she sometimes tucks extra pieces "under her chin" between her head and first pair of legs. Then she flies back to her home, chewing on the pieces. When she spreads out the mixture, it dries to a tough paper.

It is a mystery how she determines

Where can wasp nests be found? where she will place her new home. Often it is on the end of a tree branch or under the roof of a house. But sometimes she chooses strange places. One wasp nest was built high on a factory chimney, next to the whistle. Everytime the whistle blew, hundreds of wasps buzzed in all directions. Another nest was made in a car that had been in a used-car lot all summer. Still another was built over a schoolhouse door. School couldn't be opened in September until the wasp nest was removed from its unusual location.

What is the difference between a wasp

What is a hornet? and a hornet? Hornets are short, active wasps that live by the hundreds in their paper nest. "Yellowjackets" and "white-faced hornets" are actually special kinds of wasps.

Just like the bees, there are workers, drones and queens. But most wasp paper palaces last only a few months. On the other hand, a beehive may last for years.

The queen chews the wood until it makes a sticky paste. Then she plasters it on the underside of a branch or roof or the interior of an animal's den. Even a family of skunks has to move out when the wasps move in.

She makes a little six-sided paper cell. It is shallow at first and hangs downward. She places a single egg in

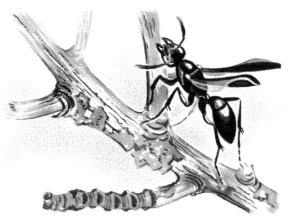

A Polistes queen scrapes wood to make paper.

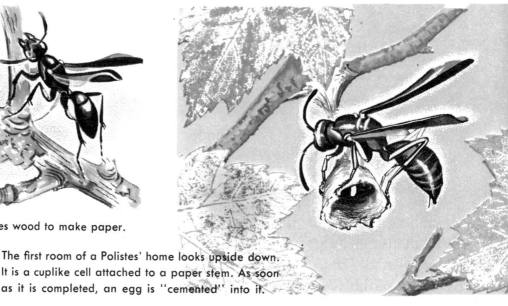

The first room of a Polistes' home looks upside down. It is a cuplike cell attached to a paper stem. As soon as it is completed, an egg is "cemented" into it.

the cell, covered with a sticky material so it won't fall out. A few more cells and eggs complete her little nest.

When the larvae hatch out, they are

How do baby wasps live? legless and blind like the bee larvae. Often they have sticky "glue pads" on them to hold them in their upside-down cradle. Their mother catches flies and other insects to feed them. She chews up the insects into a little ball. Then she holds the ball down where the babies can feed on it. She puts it first into one cell and then another until it is all gone. Each larva has a few bites. Then the mother flies away for more insect food with which to feed her larvae.

As her larvae get bigger, she keeps adding to the length of the cells. Finally, her half-dozen youngsters emerge as adult wasps. Sometimes the mother is killed before they complete their growth. Then a little empty wasp nest is all that remains to show where she had started housekeeping.

The new wasps help their mother. They

How do the new wasps help in the nest? build more cells until they have a big, flat layer of them. Then they add a second layer below that, separated from the "floor" above. There may be a dozen layers in the completed nests, each layer having several hundred cells. When they are filled with larvae, and the workers are hunting for food, all the insects around the nest are in danger.

Sometimes a cow in a pasture will walk close to a hornet nest. As she goes slowly by, eating the grass, the hornets discover the flies buzzing around her. One by one they pick them off, never hurting the cow at all. In fact, the cow doesn't even seem to notice them.

As the nest gets larger, the workers build a paper bag around it. This may be of many layers and it serves as insulation. It keeps out noontime heat and the cold of evening. It also serves as a "raincoat" for the nest. Sometimes, if the wood came from a painted building, it may be streaked with colors. Some

Strange-looking larvae, hanging upside down, hatch from the Polistes' eggs. They are fed with chewed caterpillars (above). At right, the finished "paper palace"; a Polistes' nest, showing many chambers, and adult wasps.

paper wasps may build nests three or four feet across, containing thousands of insects.

There is one question which still puzzles scientists. Honey-bees feed royal jelly to a larva to produce a queen, but how are queen wasps produced? They are not grown in oversize cells, nor are they given special food. Yet a large colony may have several queens, all getting along together and all laying eggs in the empty cells.

How are queen wasps produced?

Some scientists think they may have the answer. Wasps lick each other, just as the other social insects do. Perhaps some special material from an egg-

BALD-FACED HORNET

WORKER   QUEEN

DRONE

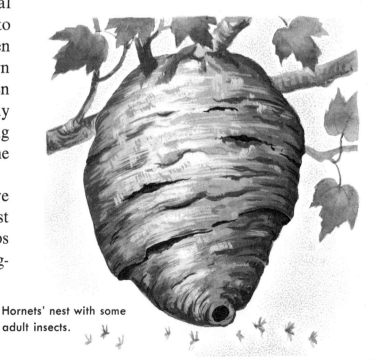

Hornets' nest with some adult insects.

YELLOW JACKET

Cutaway view of the nest of a tropical wasp.

her own, so no more queens will grow until the hive is much larger. But this has not been proved.

What happens to the wasps in the fall?

Autumn is approaching. The queens are not laying so many eggs. Some of them are laid without being fertilized by the male sperm, which the queens have stored in their bodies. These turn into drones. Like drone bees, they cannot sting. They visit flowers and ripened fruit, drinking the sweet liquids. As with the drone bees, they are waiting for the coming of new queens.

Now more queens hatch out. They fly into the air and mate with the drones. They circle around the nest for a while and then leave their paper palace. The workers, too, spend more time flying around and less time in feeding the babies.

People in the country ask in the fall, "Where are all the wasps coming from?" Of course, they have been in their nests all along, but now they are no longer doing their household duties. Their days in the sun will be cut short with the first frost. Then they will fall lifeless to earth. Only the new queens will remain — safely hidden under a bit of bark — to start a new paper palace in the spring.

laying queen is passed around in the licking process. This prevents other wasps from laying eggs by acting on their systems in some way. But when a nest gets too large, only a little bit of the queen's material goes to each worker. Finally one is able to lay eggs. Now she begins to produce material of

ANTS

We have learned that there are species of wasps and bees that do not live in societies, but are solitary insects. There are, however, no solitary ants. Even the most primitive kinds are organized into communities, and the ants are the most highly developed species of the insect world.

Like the bees and wasps that live in communities, the ants have classes, or castes, among the adults. Like bees, the workers are females, mostly unable to lay eggs, but their occupations are more numerous than those in the bee society. The worker is usually much smaller than the queen and has no wings. Ant queens and males have wings which they use in their mating flight and while searching for new colony sites.

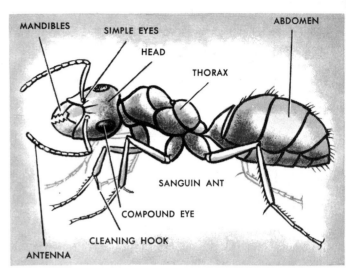
An ant looks like three insects pinned together.

Sanguin ants use their antennae to communicate.

The Forest of Grass

Day after day the hundreds of large new queens and little drones have made their way toward the entrance to the ant hill. But each time something seemed to stop them. Sometimes it would be a mass of workers dragging in a dead

When do the winged ants fly?

Cross section through a sanguin ant's body. The crop, located in the abdomen just in front of the stomach, is actually a second stomach and one of the most unusual parts of the ant's anatomy. All food is first collected in this crop. From here, the ant presses food back in her mouth to feed the queen or the other ants that have stayed at home. If the ant needs nourishment herself, she has to press food from the crop into her own stomach. The cleaning hooks on the front legs are used exclusively for cleaning of the antennae. Clean antennae provide "good reception."

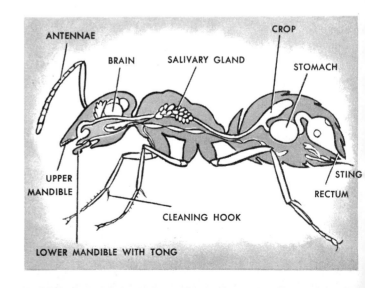

beetle. Sometimes the workers themselves would bar the way. But today, with the sun shining on the summer meadows, it is different.

Like the swarming bees or the paperwasps in the fall, the ants lay aside their daily work. Workers and soldiers rush back and forth. They wave their antennae and push each other. Sometimes a huge soldier picks up a little worker and carries her around for half an hour. In the middle of it all the queens and drones flutter their untried wings.

The activity spills outside the nest, like boiling water from a kettle. One after the other the winged ones climb up sticks and blades of grass. They stretch their new wings for a moment — and are gone. Up into the air they go, until they are tiny points of light in the sunshine. They have left the nest forever. The wingless workers that have followed them to the tips of the grass blades now turn back toward the ant hill below.

All around are the chattering birds.

Who are their enemies? Robber flies and dragonflies dart back and forth. Spiders find their webs filled with dozens of new victims. The whole meadow is filled with activity, for hundreds of nests have sent out their little aviators at once. Now the birds and other creatures are having a feast.

A heavy-bodied queen has flown above the trees at the edge of the field. She meets a drone one-third her size. They mate in the air. Then, like the drone bee, the male flutters dying to the ground.

The new queen glides to a landing.

What does the queen do with her wings? Then she does an astounding thing. Hooking her legs up over those shiny wings, she twists the wings until they break off.

One after the other, the wings fall to

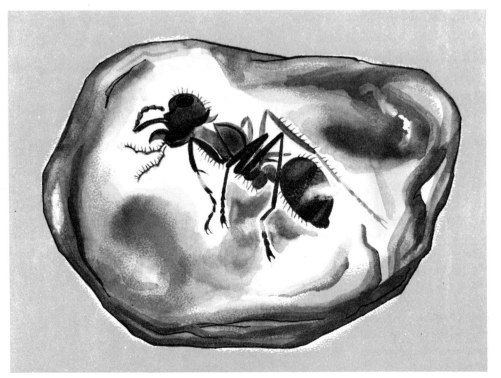

Most animals changed considerably in the course of millions of years of the earth's history. Many became extinct. But the ants have survived and changed only little, as is apparent from this early specimen, trapped and preserved in resin millions of years ago.

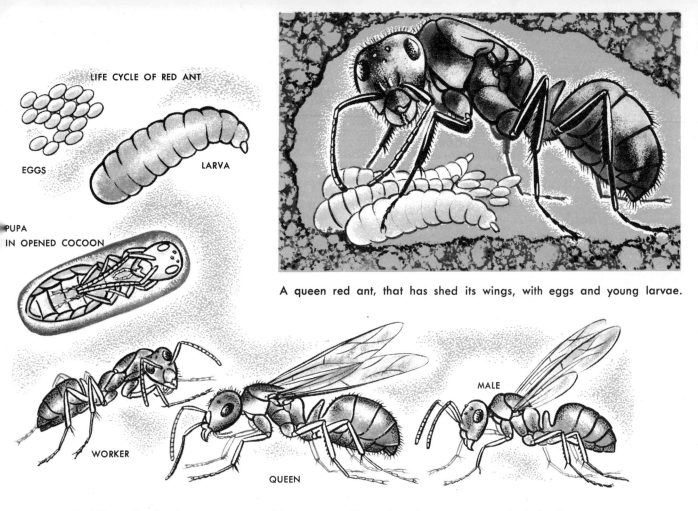

LIFE CYCLE OF RED ANT

EGGS

LARVA

PUPA
IN OPENED COCOON

A queen red ant, that has shed its wings, with eggs and young larvae.

WORKER

QUEEN

MALE

earth. Now she looks strange and hump-backed. Her huge muscles no longer have any wings to operate. But they will soon have another job to do.

She hunts quickly for a place to hide. Burrowing under a stone, she digs into the earth. There she makes a little chamber and seals it tight. Alone in the dark, she begins her new family.

Here is where her great wing-muscles are put to work again. They begin to shrink, giving their nourishment back to her body. As she absorbs their strength, she lays half a dozen eggs. In a day or two a few more are produced. Finally she has a little cluster of eggs.

Sealed in her chamber, how can she find any food? There are no workers to help her gather insects or crumbs. When the first larvae hatch in a few days, what will there be for them to eat?

But food is near at hand. Strange as it seems, the queen picks out an egg and feeds it to a newly-hatched larva, then another egg to another larva, and so on. The little babies, half-starved on such a limited diet, can hardly survive. She gives them saliva from her mouth, but they are still so tiny that it seems they will shortly die.

What do the new larvae eat?

Finally, they form little cocoons. Some of them starve before they emerge. At last, perhaps a month or two after the first egg was laid, a single worker comes out. She is joined by three or four more. Called "minims" because of their tiny size, they are the only hope for a new ant colony. Their mother's strength is nearly gone. They break

What are "minims"?

through the walls of the chamber. Out in the sunshine, they find the food that is so badly needed. Carrying it back, they give it to their mother.

When she is stronger, she lays more eggs.

What kind of nests do ants build?

The larvae are cared for by the little workers, and they continue to grow bigger and stronger. When they turn into workers themselves, they may be twice as large as their older sisters. They may live six months or more — far longer than the little minims. Then they take care of still bigger and stronger larvae. A nursery is hollowed out for the brood of larvae. Carpenter ants cut galleries in wood. Meadow ants make their homes under the earth. Woodland ants build huge ant hills of sticks and soil. Each kind of ant builds its special home.

Ant hills are more than just piles of dirt thrown out by the ants. They are filled with tunnels and passageways. As the sun hits the hill, the nurses bring the larvae up into the warm soil. If it gets too hot, they are moved over to the shaded side. If it is too cold, they are brought nearer the surface.

Around the home of the ant is a forest of grass.

How do ants find their way?

Each leaf and stone is a part of her world. Scientists think she can recognize them by sight. She goes out in the "forest" each day to find food for her colony. She finds her way by following the scent left by her sisters. She may use the same

HARVESTER
ANT
WITH SEED

LITTLE
BLACK ANTS

trail for long distances, sometimes a hundred feet or more, and she may travel it for five or six years. Ants have the longest life span of any insects.

Often they keep their little grass forest as clean as a city park. Each day they carry away bits of food that have been left behind. They toss aside sticks and pebbles. They sweep the ground with their front feet. They even cut the grass near the nest entrance, like gardeners mowing a lawn.

Down beneath the surface, the nest is always active.

How do ant larvae live?

The little larvae are shaped like the letter "j." They are carried from one nursery to another by the workers. Sometimes a worker carries six or eight of them at once. Their sticky bodies cling together. She puts them on a piece of food, leaving them to eat like little sheep put out to pasture. Then she may walk right on top of them as she goes back for more.

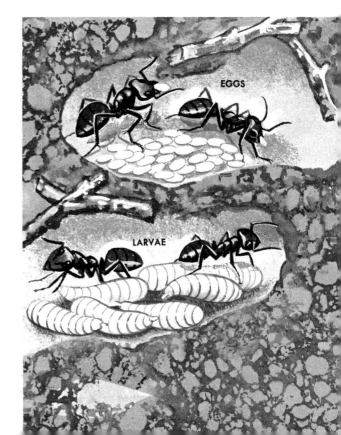

EGGS

LARVAE

Finally, after several days, the ant larvae spin tiny cocoons. A few of them are larger than the others, while a few more are smaller. Within these special cocoons a wonderful thing is happening. The pupae are growing their own magic carpets — four shining wings which will carry their owners far above the nest.

Of all the thousands of ants in the ant hill, only these few special ones can enjoy the freedom of flight. They are the new queens and drones.

Some queen ants live for sixteen or **How long do queen ants live?** eighteen years. They may move every few weeks, like the army ants, or they may spend years in the same nest. But even the most stay-at-home ants may move to a new spot. What decides when and where they will move? This is just one of the questions about ants that still waits for an answer.

While bees eat only nectar and pollen, **What do ants eat?** ants eat many things. They eat nectar if they can get it, but pollen is too hard for their taste. They eat insects and the sweet juices of fruit. Seeds of grasses and berries are also a part of their diet.

FIRE ANT

ARMY ANT

When an ant comes across a large supply of food, it rushes **How do ants tell others about food?** back to the nest. Waving its antennae and striking with its feet, it whacks every ant in its path. It pushes them away from whatever they are doing. Such unusual behavior sets them to doing the same thing, until they are all jostling and shoving. Sometimes they even butt each other with their heads, like little goats. Soon the nest looks as if it were a free-for-all fight.

CARPENTER ANT

Now they begin to spill out of the nest, still pushing and shoving. They run around in little circles and zigzag lines. Sooner or later a few find the food. Then the pushing starts all over again as soon as they get back home. This may keep up until the food is gone.

Sometimes several ants find a chunk of food at once, and try to bring it back to the nest. Most of them pull in the right direction, but a few do not. They tug north while the rest tug south. Some even get on top and tug upward!

ECITON ANT

PHARAOH'S ANT

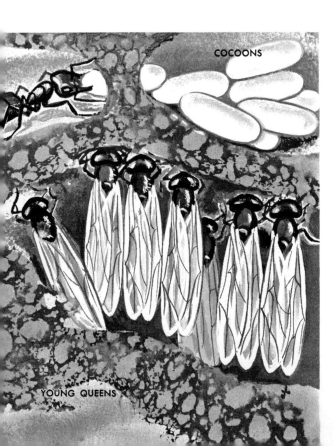

COCOONS

YOUNG QUEENS

Ants usually keep their young of different ages in different rooms. Here is a formica ants' nest with a group of winged young queens, eggs, cocoons and larvae, all separated and cared for by workers.

35

The army ants are nomadic and have no permanent nests. They move in large columns, carrying along eggs, larvae and cocoons.

Army ant workers, a third the size of "royalty," attend a queen.

Armies on the March

Something is happening in the forest.

How do the army ants live? There is a soft rustling sound on the forest floor. It is almost like the falling of distant rain. The jungle animals are behaving strangely. At the edge of a clearing, mice and lizards run ahead — and then stop. Then they run again.

Several birds are flying over a dark, soft-looking carpet, catching insects that leap into the air. The "carpet" moves slowly ahead.

An army of ants is on the march. Hundreds of thousands of workers cut and slice at everything that moves.

ARGENTINE ANT

CORNFIELD ANT

Coming across a grasshopper, they force it to jump. But it may jump in the wrong direction and land right in the middle of them. They quickly cut it in pieces. Then they send the chunks back toward the end of the line where the larvae are waiting to be fed. This is the family without a home, the gypsy band of the tropics. Even jungle cats and huge snakes flee from the fierce attack of these ants.

Somewhere in the rear of the army is the queen. Like the queen honeybee, she is a prisoner, although there are no walls around her. She is so heavy with eggs that she would be helpless by her-

A fierce little army ant attacks a much larger tarantula, and usually wins the fight.

self. As fast as she lays eggs, they are taken away by nurse ants and cared for during the first few weeks. Larvae are hatched from these eggs. Then the larvae form pupae. Soon ants emerge as quick-running workers or huge soldiers with jaws so heavy that they cannot feed themselves.

Army ants live in the African and South American tropics. Sometimes their lines may be several hundred feet long. They are often made of two streams. One stream carries food back to the nursery, while the other is going out for more. They even climb to wasp nests and attack the grubs in their paper cells. The wasps are completely helpless against such huge numbers of ferocious enemy ants.

There are about fifteen thousand species of ants known. Like the army ants, most

How many kinds of ants are known?

of them hunt and wage war, although they are not so easily seen. From the tiny, yellow, kitchen "grease ant," so small that it can hide under a grain of sugar, to the huge Brazilian Ponerine ant that is over an inch long, they live from one battle to the next. Even those that do not catch other insects for food have to defend their nests against many enemies.

Sometimes hunting ants bring back

What ants have slaves? other ant pupae to be slaves. After these emerge, they take care of their new stepbrothers and sisters as if they were their own family. They may even go into battle against members of their old nest, but they are raised to take over much of the work in the nest for their masters.

Sometimes farmers use hunting ants as

How are some ants useful? insect traps. In the tropics, some of them live in logs or hollow vines. The farmer places the nest in an orchard tree. The hunters clean out every insect. Then the farmer moves the nest to another tree, or makes a "bridge" of sticks for the ants to cross from one tree to another. Soon a whole section of orchard is free of insects.

Some ants are farmers themselves. The

What are ant farmers? leafcutting ants of South and Central America raise mushrooms for food. They snip pieces of leaves from trees and bushes and carry them along over their heads like little umbrellas. Back at the nest, they bury them deep underground. Soon a special fungus grows on them that the ants use for food. When a queen ant starts a new home, she takes a bit of this fungus with her.

"Go to the ant, thou sluggard," said King Solomon in the Bible. "Consider her ways and be wise." He was probably thinking of another ant farmer, the harvester. When the seeds are ripe, the harvesters carry them to the nest. Long lines of ants can be seen in the Middle East, each ant carrying a seed.

Then the ants set up a "chewing society." Hour after hour they chew on the seeds. Chemicals in their saliva help change the starch of the seeds to sugar. Then this "ant bread" is fed to the larvae.

Many ants eat the sweet substance

How do ants keep "cows"? called "honeydew." It comes from aphids or plant lice as they feed on the sap of plants. The ant strokes

CARPENTER
ANT
IN WOOD

FIRE ANT

This cross section through the nest of the garden ants shows the mound of earth thrown up by the insects. Passages lead deep into the ground where the real nest lies.

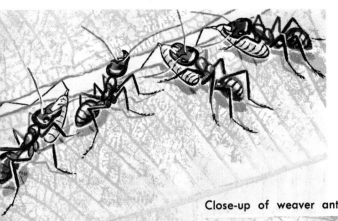

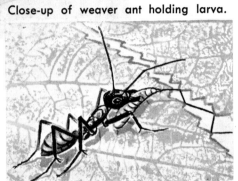

Close-up of weaver ant holding larva.

Above, some weaver ants hold two leaves, while behind the leaves other ants, holding larvae which secrete a thread, "stitch" the leaves together to build their nest.

Finished nest of the weaver ant, built from leaves woven together.

the aphid almost as if it were a farmer milking a cow. The aphid gives out a little drop of honeydew. Sometimes the ants will even pick up the aphids in their jaws and carry them to a new spot. Other times, if the honeydew is not coming fast enough, the ant may go ahead and eat the whole aphid.

In the southwestern United States the

What are honey ants? strange honey ants have their living storage jars. They go out to search for the nectar from flowers. Coming back to the nest, they give the nectar to a young ant, called a "callow," whose body is still soft and flexible. She hangs by her hind legs from the roof of a little underground room. Larger and larger she gets, until she is round and clear, like a little yellow marble. Then she serves as a storage jar for her sisters. Sometimes she hangs there as long as three years — sometimes shorter. If the honey ants give the callow too much nectar, she bursts.

Little underground gardens, aphid

How do ants protect their nests? "cows" and living honeypots attract enemies. But the workers have many ways of fighting them. Although workers cannot fly, the "bulldog" ants of Australia can jump. Sometimes they leap a foot into the air. Many ants have fiery stings. Some bite with their jaws and then spray a burning fluid from their bodies into the wound. Some even use little "squirt guns." Pointing the end of their bodies upward, they squirt out a drop of liquid.

Ant hills may be eight feet high. The

How large are ant hills? "gardens" of the fungus-growing leafcutters may be seven feet beneath the surface. But the largest families and the largest homes do not belong to the ants at all. They belong to the termites, sometimes wrongly called "white ants." Their story will be told in the next chapter.

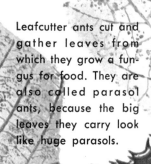

Leafcutter ants cut and gather leaves from which they grow a fungus for food. They are also called parasol ants, because the big leaves they carry look like huge parasols.

The fragments of the leaves are chewed up in the nest and mixed with saliva for the "garden." But leafcutter ants do not feed on the leaves.

CLOSE-UP OF A HONEYPOT ANT

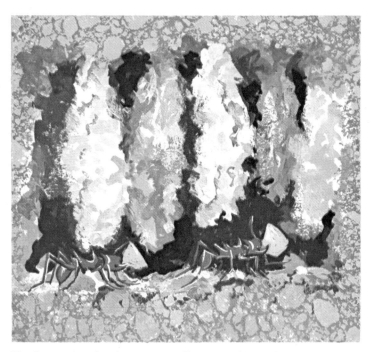

The fungus garden is a sponge-like mass that is full of passages. It is situated in a special chamber of the nest, far under the ground.

The desert ant uses some members of the colony as storage containers, filled to the bursting point with sweet juices. They are hung up in specially constructed chambers. During the lean months, when the galls on which desert ants normally feed do not provide a regular diet, the ants feed from their honey-juice "storage containers."

Ants stroke aphids, little plant lice, with their antennae and squeeze a drop of honeydew out of their abdomens — like farmers milking cows.

TERMITES

The Wooden Cavern

The newborn termite struggles with a piece of wood.

What are newborn termites like?

The chunk, chewed off by a worker a few minutes before, is twice the baby's size. But the baby moves the wood from the center of the dark tunnel. Then it goes along to find another job. In the termite nest, even the babies go to work.

Unlike the larvae of the bees, wasps and ants, the young termite can get around all by itself. It trots around on its six legs, not needing a nursery or a protecting cell. Called a *nymph,* it looks like a miniature copy of the adults all around it.

At first it needs special food. It stops the older termites

What food does it eat?

which pump up some of the food from their stomachs. Even the males take part in the process, for the male termites work as hard as the females.

As the little termite gets older, its taste for food changes. It begins to gnaw on the sides and walls of its home, which is often hollowed out of wood. It will live on wood and plant material for the rest of its life.

Strange as it seems, the termite cannot digest its own food. Good, un-rotted wood

How is a termite's food digested?

must be digested for it. Inside its body are little creatures called *protozoa.* When the termite sends a load of food down to them, these tiny chemists get to work. They break the wood down into

Termite mounds, especially those in the tropics, are often very high. This one is an African termite mound, taller than the average man.

41

simpler material — and finally to sugar. Then the termite absorbs the sugar into its own bloodstream. Some kinds of termites live without these tiny helpers, but they do not feed on sound wood. Their food is rotten wood, fungus and decayed material.

The newborn termite has no protozoa in its digestive system. Yet it needs them before it will be able to digest wood. It probably gets protozoa by the "living lollipop" method of licking its neighbors and passing food back and forth. Like all insects, it sheds its skin for growth. At the same time, it loses its protozoa. But after it has licked a few neighbors, the protozoa are back.

VO TERMITES
CTUAL SIZE)

Why are termite nests closed?

Day after day the nymph works in the darkness with thousands of its brothers and sisters. If an accident takes place so that the nest is opened, they quickly seal it up again. Making a paste of saliva and sawdust, they build a new wall. Soon

the nest is cool and dark. But it is not the light that disturbs them, for they are blind. The dryness of the outside air would soon kill them, as they need dampness for life.

Termites in houses are careful not to eat right through the wood so that air gets inside their tunnels. This is why it is so hard to know if termites are present. The wood looks the same, whether they are there or not. Only by testing to see if it is solid can one be sure. Sometimes they eat up from the cellar to attic without once breaking out into the open. If they come to a bookshelf, they may eat the shelf and the inside pages of all the books!

How long do termites live?

The nymph may live six or seven years. If it is going to become a queen or king, little bumps begin to show on its back or thorax. These are the buds of the new wings. If it is just a worker, the bumps never develop. With each shedding of the skin the buds get larger, until the termite reaches its full growth. Then it waits in the nest for the day of flight. Sometimes it may wait six years in desert country.

What is a termite "flight day"?

Nobody knows what makes a "flight day" for termites. But suddenly they appear by the thousands. They resemble flying ants, although their waists are thicker and they have equal-sized wings. Ants have thinner waists, and the front wings

The wings of the termite queen look as if they were made out of a very delicate lace.

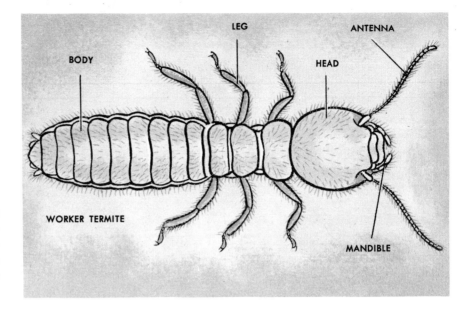

BODY   LEG   ANTENNA   HEAD   WORKER TERMITE   MANDIBLE

Compare this illustration with the one on page 31. It shows why the termite, which is often called the white ant, is as far removed from the white ant as a horse is from a hippopotamus. Their bodies are built differently, the larvae develop differently and the organization of the societies is different. A termite is not a white ant.

are longer than the rear ones. Like ants, they break off the wings when they reach the ground again.

Now a strange thing happens. The female termite raises the tip of her body high into the air. Special scent glands send an odor on the breeze. The wind carries it to a male termite. He cannot fly to meet her, for his wings are broken off, too. So he struggles over sticks and pebbles until he reaches her. Greeting each other by touching their antennae, they find a crack in a log or rotten stump. Then they disappear to mate and start a new home.

Of all the social insects, only the ter-

How long do royal termites live?

mites have a king. All the other queens are widows, for they have lost their husbands on the mating flight. The termite family gets started very slowly, sometimes with only a few nymphs the first year. But the royal couple is not in a hurry. They are surrounded by food — and they are the longest-lived of all insects. Some scientists believe they may live as long as forty years.

The queen gets larger and larger. Her

Why is the queen called an egg-machine?

body becomes little more than a huge sack of eggs. They are produced one after another. Soon she is little more than an egg-laying machine. Workers feed her at one end and take the eggs away from the other!

The steeple-termite of Africa makes one

How large are termite houses?

of the largest insect homes on earth. It may be more than fifteen feet high and built of sand and sawdust mixed with saliva. The royal couple lives inside in its own chamber. The king's egg-filled mate is as big as a sausage. She may lay ten million eggs a year.

Perhaps the young nymph is growing

What are soldier termites?

up to be a soldier instead of a king, queen or worker. With each molt, its head grows larger and harder. Its jaws get stronger. Soon it seems to be all head. It helps protect the termites against their enemies, the

43

insect-eating ants. If there is a break in the nest, the soldiers rush to that point, their jaws snapping and clicking. They knock their heads against the sides of the galleries. This sets all the termites in motion; soon the hole is repaired.

Some termites have another kind of soldier called a "nasute." **What is a "nasute"?** It has a little nozzle on the front of its head. When enemies come, the soldier squirts a messy liquid from the nozzle.

A worker ant, bee or wasp has little chance of ever laying any eggs. But worker or soldier termites sometimes become "second queens." They never get as fat as their huge mother, but they may mate with a male in the nest and start their own egg-factory.

About two thousand species of termites are known. **How many kinds of termites are there?** Some of them have their own little fungus gardens on decayed leaves underground, like the gardening ants. Others build homes in trees, with tunnels leading back down to the soil. Some have underground tunnels one hundred fifty feet

WORKERS

SOLDIER

KING

KING AND SOLDIER

long. Still others build homes with sawdust umbrellas on top.

But even stranger than the termites are the creatures that live with them, for a termite nest contains odd little guests. So do ant hills, beehives and hornet nests. Some are "beggars" and some are "thieves." The story of insect intruders that force their way into the nests of other insects will be told in the next chapter.

INSECT INTRUDERS

Quietly the little wax-moth makes her way into the beehive. **How can a moth destroy a honeycomb?** If the bees find her, they will kill her. The wax-moth lays a few eggs in the hive and flies away.

Soon the eggs hatch. The caterpillars make their way to the comb. They begin to eat the wax, tunneling through it as they go. They leave little silk threads and bits of garbage. Soon the wonderful comb is ruined.

EGGS

QUEEN

A bee comes into the hive with three or four little flies clinging to her. They have no wings of their own.

What are some of the other hive-robbers?

They use the bee like an airplane to take them from place to place. When they get into the hive, they lay their eggs. The tiny larvae eat the wax cap of the bee cradles. When they turn into adult flies, they get aboard another insect airplane.

Sometimes a bee brings in the larva of the oil beetle. This became attached while the bee was visiting a flower for nectar. Now the larva goes crawling to the brood comb. Here it feeds on the bee's eggs before they hatch. Growing larger, the larva steals honey. When it turns into an adult oil beetle, it leaves the beehive.

Wasp families have their visitors, too. Some Vespula wasps of Europe are hard-working paper builders.

What insects invade nests of wasps?

But a Vespula queen of another species may come along. She enters the nest, fights with the true queen and finally kills her. Soon she is laying her own eggs. After a few weeks, the nest is made up of the new Vespula species.

Wasps sometimes have a little garbage-disposal force. These are the larvae of the common clothes moth. They feed on the empty skins of insects that have been dropped by the wasps. The young of a fly, known as Volucella, feed on dead insects. However, if not enough dead ones are around, the Volucella may quietly eat a wasp grub before the workers can stop it.

Ants have the most guests and visitors. One bug, called the "paralyzer," has special tufts of hair on its body.

What is the "paralyzer"?

The ants lick the secretions from them, but they soon lose control of their muscles. Then the bug feeds on the ants with its pointed beak.

Kidnap-beetles, or rove beetles, hide in the tunnels of ant nests. When a larva is carried past, the beetle snatches it right out of the worker's jaws.

What are some other ant visitors?

Then the beetle races for shelter with its catch. If the ant

WINGED MALE AND NYMPH

WASP ENEMIES

VOLUCELLA

VESPULA

WAX-MOTH

OIL BEETLE

BEE ENEMIES

LARVA OF OIL BEETLE

VOLUCELLA

CHALCID FLY

ATEMELES BEETLE

ANT ENEMIES

LOMECHUSA BEETLE AND LARVA

way into another ant hill. She snips off the head of the real queen. The ants, without a queen, soon adopt her. They raise her eggs and young. Bit by bit, as the old ants die off, the nest turns into a family of beheading ants.

Some rove beetles seem to have such a pleasant taste that the ants neglect their own brood. They feed and lick the beetles known as Lomechusa. They give them the food that should go to the ant larvae. Meanwhile, the Lomechusa grubs feast on the young ants. After a while the ant hill may die.

Even the blind, dark-loving termites **What creatures live in termite homes?** have their little guests. The white mite is a tiny creature. It runs all over the backs and bodies of the termites. When one termite feeds another, the mite is right at hand. It points its beak right into the bubble of food going between them. For some reason the termites don't seem to mind it.

Termite mounds have beetles and bugs **What is a Jerrymunglum?** of many types. Ants are forever attacking them, too. But two of the termite's worst enemies live right in the walls of the mounds. One is the termite lizard that snaps up every termite it finds. The other is the sun spider or Jerrymunglum. This creature, about three-quarters of an inch long, looks like a brown, hairy spider. Its jaws are like pliers. It forces its way right through the walls of termite tunnels. Then it feeds on the termites.

Why do social insects allow all these

chases it, the beetle squirts an unpleasant fluid in the ant's face.

Even the terrible army ants have their camp-followers. Beetles and bugs go along on ant raids. Many of them are shaped like the ants themselves. Probably this keeps them safe from attack. When food is sent back to the queen and the nurses, the camp-followers help themselves. The army ants are blind and probably cannot tell the difference.

The beheading ant queen forces her

creatures to live in their nests? Most of them have a taste or odor that the insects seem to like. But this may not be the complete answer.

In the next chapter you will learn how to make your own insect zoo. Then, perhaps, you may find some of the answers yourself.

YOUR INSECT ZOO

Honeybees are fascinating to watch. Perhaps you know of someone who has a hive of his own. A high school biology teacher may be able to help you get an "observation hive." This is a little glass-walled bee colony. Put it in a bright place away from direct sunlight. Then you can watch the bees at work.

How can you watch bees at home?

What do you feed your captive honeybees? Just leave the window open a half-inch and they will feed themselves. Flying away from their new home, they disappear into the sky. Half an hour later they return, loaded with pollen and nectar.

Wasp nests are best left where you find them. But you can still enjoy watching them if you have a pair of binoculars. You will see them bringing flies and other insects.

How can you watch wasps?

The underside of roofs and sheltered walls are good places to find mud-dauber wasps. They pay no attention to you if you watch them quietly. Then you will see them bringing spiders to their mud nests. These will serve as food for their newly-hatched larvae.

Sand wasps can be followed as they drag caterpillars along the ground to their holes. Even little plant galls can be brought into the house and kept in a closed jar until the tiny wasps hatch.

An observation ant home is called a *formicarium*. It can be made of two panes of glass separated by strips of wood around the edges. Then, if a small ant hill is dug up carefully, you will find the humpbacked queen. Put her in a jar with some of her workers, larvae and cocoons. You will probably discover that you have some of the strange ant guests, too. Carefully place them all in the formicarium.

How can you make a nest for ants?

No soil is needed for your ant nest. Before you seal it up, place a sponge near one edge for moisture. Drill two holes in the wood for two medicine droppers. One is to wet the sponge, and the other is for honey, water and melted butter with a little egg white. This will serve as food for the ants. Then the panes are taped together.

Keep the nest covered with dark paper except when looking at the ants. A piece of red cellophane or glass will

WOOD

TAPE

GLASS

EYE DROPPER

FOOD

WATER

A formicarium with earth between the panes of glass offers a good opportunity to study the interesting life of ants.

let you watch without disturbing them. You will see the ants feeding their queen and caring for their young.

If you wish to watch termites, pull apart an old stump or log until you find a family of these insects. Then search carefully for the large king and his larger queen. Put the family in a darkened jar. Add bits of the wood and laboratory filter paper for food. Keep a moist sponge in the jar. There is little danger of your termites getting away, as they would die soon after they left the moisture of the nest.

How can termites be kept?

The best insect zoo, however, is the one that is right outdoors. With a magnifying glass you can watch the insects at work in their own homes. Even a city park has

What is the best insect zoo of all?

its ants, bees, wasps and termites. A dish of honey on a window sill will soon attract the bees. Mud placed nearby will be found by mud-dauber wasps. Chunks of soft wood will be chewed up by the paper wasps for their homes. A bouquet of flowers in a glass of water will attract insect visitors.

In your outdoor zoo you can watch the ants in their ceaseless battles. You may see other battles, too, for social insects will fight with any insect that is not from their own nest.

You can watch a fighting ant with its abdomen bitten off, still fighting. You can drop a piece of paper on the scent-trail of the ants and watch them try to find the way again. You can learn which colors most attract bees.

There are many other things you can find out yourself. When you see something interesting, write it down. Soon you will have a book of your own.

THE HOW AND WHY WONDER BOOK OF
REPTILES
AND AMPHIBIANS

By ROBERT MATHEWSON, Curator of Science,
Staten Island Institute of Arts and Sciences, Staten Island, N. Y.
Illustrated by DOUGLAS ALLEN and DARRELL SWEET
Editorial Production: DONALD D. WOLF

Edited under the supervision of
    Dr. Paul E. Blackwood.
    Washington, D. C.

Text and illustrations approved by
    Oakes A. White, Brooklyn Children's Museum, Brooklyn, New York

GROSSET & DUNLAP • **Publishers** • **NEW YORK**

Introduction

There are five large groups of backboned animals on earth today. They are the amphibians, birds, fishes, reptiles and mammals. This *How and Why Wonder Book* deals with two of these groups — amphibians and reptiles.

Which snakes are poisonous and which ones are not? This seems to be an endlessly interesting question to most people. Equally interesting are the fantastic superstitions and misbeliefs about snakes. This book deals with both of these topics. It tells which snakes are poisonous and which ones are not. It tells about many of the common superstitions and provides correct information about them. In addition, it tells many other interesting things about amphibians and reptiles, such as their eating habits, how they protect themselves and how they move.

In the Space Age there is no lesser need for people with knowledge about all plant and animal life. This interesting and informative book on reptiles and amphibians may stimulate a potential young scientist to select *herpetology* (the study of reptiles) as his major field of interest.

Youthful herpetologists who wish to learn about the habits of reptiles by close observation will be glad to know that several of the reptiles make good pets. This *How and Why Wonder Book* tells which ones may easily be kept as pets and gives suggestions for collecting and keeping them.

Paul E. Blackwood

Dr. Blackwood is a professional employee in the U. S. Office of Education. This book was edited by him in his private capacity and no official support or endorsement by the Office of Education is intended or should be inferred.

Library of Congress Catalog Card Number: 60-51569

CONTENTS

VARANOSAURUS

EDAPHOSAURUS

The Age of Reptiles

In the beginning, warm seas flooded over much of the land, and there was life only in the water. During certain times of the year, the pools and lakes in which these sea creatures lived dried up, and many of the animals perished. But after millions of years, some of these creatures developed the ability to breathe dry air, and they became able to spend part of their lives on the land. These creatures were called amphibians, a name which comes from the Greek word meaning "two lives."

Many amphibians eventually began to spend more of their lives on land, and in time, they became better adapted to it. Finally, some of these creatures became able to live on the land all of the time, and these land-living animals were called reptiles, which comes from a Latin word meaning "crawler."

During the early Mesozoic period in the history of the earth, about 200 million years ago, the reptiles became the most important group of animals. Other reptile forms developed, including giant

4

DIMETRODONS

dinosaurs which roamed the land, great sea reptiles and dragon-like creatures which flew. The dinosaurs became so large and powerful that they ruled the world for more than 100 million years.

But the earth was changing. The climate, which had been warm, became cool. The swampy lands grew dry. The plant life on which dinosaurs had fed began to disappear. They were cold-blooded creatures and couldn't stand the cooler temperatures, and their huge size usually prevented them from seeking shelter in smaller caves. Plant-eating dinosaurs either couldn't find enough to eat or were unable to eat the newer kinds of plants. And when the plant-eaters died, the meat-eating dinosaurs were left without a source of food. The giant dinosaurs were not able to change, or adapt, with the changing world and eventually, they died out.

Although the giant reptiles died out, smaller forms did not and their relatives survive to this day. Why they survived is not certain. Perhaps the smaller reptiles were able to adapt to the changing conditions in the world.

Today, the living reptiles include the snakes, lizards, turtles, crocodilians (alligators, crocodiles and their relatives) and the tuatara.

Getting to Know the Reptiles

SCALY SKIN

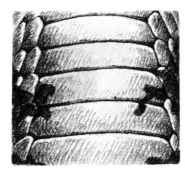

PLATED SKIN

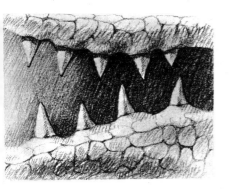

REPTILE TEETH

COPPERHEAD HATCHING

Reptiles are vertebrates (backboned animals) which live in warm climates. They are cold-blooded and the temperature of their bodies is about the same as the temperature about them. Their skin is either smooth or scaly, or covered with shells or plates. Reptiles have lungs and breathe air. Their teeth are usually uniform in shape and size. They lay eggs or bear living young which look just like the adult reptiles.

A group of boys, one of whom dangled a snake by its tail, ran after several girls. This was a typical boyish prank, and perhaps some of the girls were having fun at being chased. However, their fright of the snake was real.

Many people believe that it is natural to fear snakes, because all reptiles are supposed to be slimy, poisonous, repulsive creatures. Actually they are not. Only a few species are poisonous; their bodies are dry and clean, feeling somewhat like shoe leather; and, if we stop to look, we find that they are really colorful and attractive animals.

Babies and young children who have never been shown or told that they should fear reptiles rarely have a "natural" fear of them. When a small colorful snake or lizard, or even a turtle or alligator, is offered to a child who has never been taught to fear these animals, the child almost always reaches out for the reptile, wanting to cuddle and play with this interesting "toy."

Why are some people afraid of reptiles?

Many adults claim that they were never warned against reptiles, but that they have an instinctive terror of them. It is indeed probable that if we could see back into their early youth, we would find that something or someone gave these people the fear they now have. No one is born with a fear of snakes.

It is true, of course, that some snakes are poisonous, and it would be very foolish to touch any snake if you were not positive that it was harmless.

It is claimed, by some people, that even
**Do wild animals
fear snakes?** wild animals have an instinctive fear of snakes. Experiments have been made with the young of various animals, particularly monkeys, which, as adults, show a great fear of snakes. These experiments showed that baby monkeys that had never been near a snake showed no fear when offered one. Later the same babies were put in a cage with adult monkeys. The adults became excited when a reptile was

Young animals fear snakes only when taught to fear.

brought near the cage, and from then on the baby monkeys showed fear. We can see that they were taught to fear snakes.

No animals have been the victims of
**Are all stories
about reptiles true?** more fanciful tales than have the reptiles. In fact, some of the stories are quite silly — stories such as: "There are snakes that can take their tails into their mouths and roll downhill like a hoop"; "Turtles live for a million years"; "If a snake's head is cut off, the snake will continue to live until sundown"; "There are snakes that will wrap around your legs and whip you with their tails"; "There are snakes which can milk a cow"; "Alligators, like turtles, can live almost forever." These statements are all false, of course.

A snake does not use its tail to whip man or beast.

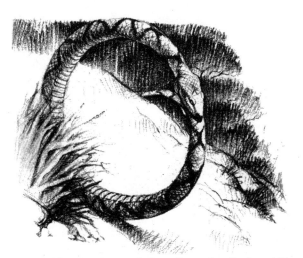
Snakes do not grasp their tails and roll downhill.

Snakes do not milk cows, goats or any other animal.

WESTERN PAINTED TURTLE

WOOD TURTLE

D.A.

BOX TURTLE

GOPHER TORTOISE

PAINTED TURTLE

LEATHERBACK TURTLE (AQUATIC)

SPOTTED TURTLE

MUD TURTLE

LOGGERHEAD TURTLE

GREEN TURTLE

SNAPPING TURTLE

Are They Poisonous or Harmless?

The fact that some snakes are poisonous

Are all snakes poisonous?

is probably one of the main reasons why people fear them. Actually most reptiles are harmless. Of the 2,450 species of snakes in the world, only 175 kinds are dangerously poisonous.

A similar situation exists with the lizards. There are only two species which are poisonous: the Mexican beaded lizard and its first cousin, the Gila monster, or Gila, of Mexico and the United States. All the hundreds of other kinds of lizards that inhabit the world are nonpoisonous. There are no poisonous turtles or crocodilians (reptiles related to, and including, the crocodiles).

Another type of reptile which is non-poisonous is the tuatara, a lizard-like animal which occurs only in New Zealand. Some scientists consider the tu-

The tuatara lives on coastal islands of New Zealand.

atara a living "fossil," because it is believed to have persisted in somewhat its present form for many millions of years.

It would be very convenient if all of the

Can you tell a poisonous snake from a harmless one?

poisonous snakes carried a "badge," or marking or shape, by which we could easily tell them from the harmless ones. All rattlesnakes are poisonous, and can be identified by a horn-like, loosely jointed rattle at the end of the tail. However, even this can be broken off accidentally.

But there is no single way by which we can tell whether an unknown snake is poisonous or harmless, unless, of course, we are willing to look into its mouth to see if it has fangs.

Some people say that if you smell

Can you locate poisonous snakes by their odor?

a cucumber odor while walking in the woodland a poisonous copperhead is nearby. To prove that this method of

The Gila gets its name from the Gila River, Arizona.

identifying snakes is risky, just ask your friends what a cucumber smells like. You will undoubtedly be given many different answers, which proves, of course, that you cannot locate copperheads or, for that matter, any snake, by their odor.

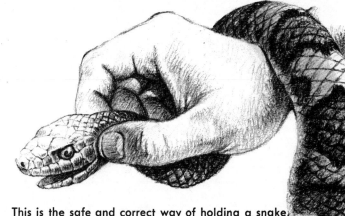

This is the safe and correct way of holding a snake.

Snake skulls: poisonous (left); nonpoisonous (right).

Another misleading belief about snakes is that if one has a triangular or diamond-shaped head it is poisonous. Some of the world's

Can you tell a poisonous snake by the shape of its head?

most dangerous snakes, including the king cobra of Malay, the black mamba of Africa and the coral snake of the United States, have blunt rounded heads. On the other hand, many of the water snakes in the United States and other countries have distinct triangle-shaped heads and are harmless. You cannot identify a poisonous snake simply by the shape of its head.

Another belief is that snakes with eyes that have round pupils are harmless, and those with elliptical pupils — like those of a cat — are

Can you tell a poisonous snake by the shape of its eyes?

poisonous. The cobras of India, Malay and Africa are all very poisonous and have eyes with round pupils, whereas the harmless night snake of the southwestern United States has elliptical pupils. So you cannot tell a poisonous snake merely by the shape of its eyes.

AFRICAN COBRA

11

BEADED LIZARD

CHUCKWALLA

WESTERN COLLARED LIZARD

Douglas Allen

DESERT SPINY LIZARD

GILA MONSTER

HORNED TOADS

One of the most popular errors about snakes is that all green-colored snakes are venomous. The green mamba of

Are green-colored snakes poisonous?

Africa is one of the most deadly snakes known, but the green snake from the northeastern United States is completely harmless; in fact, it will not even offer to bite. So all snakes that are green in color are not necessarily poisonous.

The forked tongue which many a reptile possesses is never poisonous; it merely serves as a taste organ, but not in the same way as

Is the tongue of reptiles poisonous?

ours. The reptile's tongue darts from its mouth and waves up and down, and the "taste" that is on the air is picked up. When the tongue is redrawn, the taste is wiped off as it rubs across an organ in the roof of the mouth. In this way the reptile is able to tell what is near. This is a very sensitive organ and snakes are believed to be able to detect water at great distances by this method.

The poison apparatus of the reptile consists of a set of hollow teeth (fangs), which are connected to ducts (fleshy tubes). The

Where does a snake carry its poison?

ducts, in turn, are connected to poison glands at the sides of the head. The snake has to strike or bite with these hollow teeth in order to inject the poison.

Not all snakes have the same kind of poison. Some have a somewhat similar poison, called a haemotoxin, a kind

Do all snakes have the same kind of poison?

that affects the blood. These include the rattlesnakes, copperheads and moccasins of the United States and Mexico, as well as many of the vipers, such as Wagler's and temple vipers of Malay and Russell's and Gaboon vipers of Africa.

Cobras of Africa, Malay and India, tiger snakes of Australia, and coral snakes of the southeastern United States, as well as many others, have neurotoxins, a poison which affects the nerves. Some amount of each type of poison is present in the venom of each kind of snake, so if we are to be treated for snakebite we shall have to use the serum for the particular snake that did the biting.

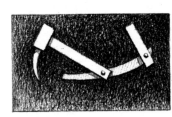

Two tubes lead from the snake's poison glands or sacs to its fangs, which are hollow. When the snake bites its victim, poison from the glands is squeezed through the fangs. The illustrations (right to left) show a rattlesnake head, skull, mechanical action of the jaws, and poison sac location (dark area). Only when injected is venom poisonous.

The twelve-foot-long boa constrictors of tropical America prey on birds and mammals.

A unique poisonous snake is the African spitting cobra. This reptile, about three to four feet in length, lives in the jungle. It not only injects its poison by biting, but when its prey or an enemy approaches, it raises its forward end off the ground and by quickly flicking the head forward, ejects small droplets of venom from the tips of its hollow fangs. At the same instant it exhales with a sharp hiss. The poison thus sprayed gets into the eyes of the victim and causes considerable harm, particularly if the eyes are rubbed.

Can snakes spit their poison?

The poisonous Gila monster and the Mexican beaded lizard do not have hollow teeth. Their venom glands are situated in the lower jaws. They cannot poison their prey unless they chew and get the venom into the victim.

How do lizards inject poison?

What Do They Eat?

The nonpoisonous snakes use other methods to catch their prey. Many are constrictors that grasp the food with their teeth and then throw loops of their bodies, in coils, around the victim. Usually, they kill not by crushing the animal, but by preventing it from breathing. Both big snakes and little snakes use this constricting method to kill their prey.

How do the nonpoisonous snakes capture their prey?

Some of the big snakes which do this are the regal python of Malay, which reaches a length of thirty feet; the twelve-foot boas and twenty-five-foot anacondas of South America; and the fifteen-foot pythons from India. Smaller ones are the mountain blacksnake from the northeastern United States and the California king snake, as well as hundreds of others.

The nonconstrictors catch their food

How do the nonconstrictors catch food?

by either grasping with the mouth and pressing the prey beneath their body or by merely swallowing it whole. All snakes swallow their food whole, because they do not have chewing or grinding teeth. Their teeth are shaped like curved needles, which hook into the prey, holding and manipulating it into the snake's throat. Their jaws are loosely connected at the skull and chin and this peculiar arrangement enables them to open their mouths very wide. Further, their overlapping body scales can be spread apart, so that bulky food can be swallowed.

A twenty-five-foot regal python can

Do they eat large animals?

easily devour a half-grown pig. A meal of this size usually takes more than an hour to swallow. Then the snake finds a suitable hiding place and may stay there more than two weeks before the meal is completely digested. The snake extends its windpipe out of the side of its mouth, like a snorkle, enabling it to breathe while eating the pig.

Lizards, turtles and crocodilians also

How do lizards catch food?

have interesting feeding habits. The African chameleon lizard captures food with its tongue. These six-to-eight-inch lizards slowly move through the bushes and trees, clasping small limbs with their clawlike feet, while their eyes are constantly searching for insects. The eyes protrude

at each side of the head and each eye can look in a different direction at the same time.

When an insect is discovered, the lizard slowly approaches until it is about its own body length away. Suddenly, with tremendous speed, the tongue shoots out and the insect disappears down the lizard's throat. The tongue is almost as long as the lizard and is tipped with a sticky, fleshy end which adheres to the prey. Almost before the insect can move, it finds itself drawn into the lizard's mouth. African chameleons have the ability to change color and usually match their surroundings so well that they are hard to find.

The American chameleon of the southeastern United States and islands of the Caribbean, while not true chameleons, can also change their body colors. These are the small lizards which are sold at the circus or pet shop. They can run very fast, and they capture insects by pouncing upon them.

How Do They Move?

Turtles move slowly as they walk, but

Can turtles move fast?

there are times when they can move very fast. The surprisingly quick lunges of the eighteen-inch common snapping turtle of the eastern United States and the large alligator snapping turtle of the Mississippi River can be dangerous, especially if we get too close to their strong jaws.

The mata mata turtle of Guiana and northern Brazil, when feeding, moves so

16

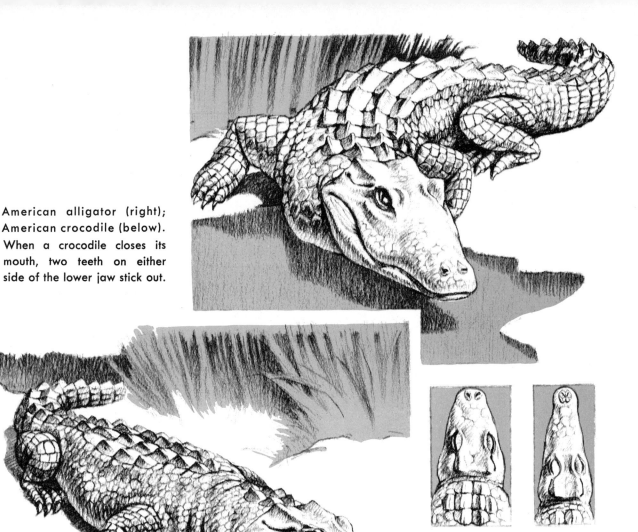

American alligator (right); American crocodile (below). When a crocodile closes its mouth, two teeth on either side of the lower jaw stick out.

Heads of alligator (left) and crocodile (right). The alligator's snout is broad and rounded while the crocodile's is pointed and its head is narrower.

fast that we can hardly follow the motion. This turtle is well camouflaged by its irregular shape and the fleshy folds of skin around the head, as well as by the water plants (algae), which are usually found growing on the shell. On discovering a small fish, the mata mata moves toward its prey ever so slowly — like a slow-motion movie. When it is about eight to ten inches from the swimming fish, it stops, and with a motion too quick to follow, its head shoots out and the open mouth sucks in the unwary food. The neck, so long that it lies folded beneath the shell, is seen to extend during this action.

Equally surprising are the movements of crocodiles and alligators. Baby crocodiles and alligators make short grunting sounds that, at times, must sound to their mothers like warning cries. When they make these sounds, the parents often race to their aid with surprising speed. Large crocodilians live in many of the tropical and sub-tropical countries

Can crocodiles and alligators move fast?

17

of the world including Africa, Mexico, Central and South America, and the southern United States. Alligator hunters say that some of these reptiles can move, for short distances, faster than a man can run.

No movement of any animal, even the lithe gait of the tiger or the wavy movements of the caterpillar, is more graceful than the slithering flow of the snake. Armless and legless, they move across the surface of

How do snakes move?

FLYING LIZARD

forward part of the body is stretched out until it touches another rough spot, such as a rock. If this spot is held with a crook of the body, the tail can then be drawn up and placed at this spot, too, and in this way, the snake's body can be pushed or pulled forward.

There are many rough spots that a snake can use and if it inches its body over all the rough spots, it then moves smoothly along the ground or appears to flow up trees. If you place a small snake upon a smooth piece of glass, its movement is similar to that of a caterpillar. These two main types of locomotion are used by most snakes.

the ground or climb trees with great ease. If we watch carefully we can soon understand how they move.

First the tail is held against a rough spot, such as a clump of grass. Then the

The sidewinder rattlesnake of the southwestern United States and the desert viper of Africa live on the soft shifting sands of the desert and, for this reason, crawl with another kind of

How do desert snakes move?

motion. By throwing loops of its body forward, the desert snake can lift the remaining part of its body off the sand, bringing it up to the forward loop. This causes it to move with a sidewinding motion, and is the reason for the name "sidewinder."

The most unusual kind of travel prac-
Can any snakes fly? ticed by snakes is used by the flying snakes of Malay. These colorful reptiles, fifteen to eighteen inches in length, are arboreal (tree-dwellers),

escape by running across the surface of the water. The toes of these lizards are provided with flaps, which are erected as the lizards run. This causes the foot to become a flat pad, which provides a surface sufficient to support their weight on top of the water. When they are far enough away from danger, they stop running and sink out of sight.

Some small desert lizards, such as the sand skink, escape their enemies by diving into loose sand. Then, by a swimming motion, they progress quite rapidly beneath the surface. The geckos, a

GECKO

Flying lizards glide from tree to tree with the aid of their folds of skin. The harmless, ridge-toed gecko gets its name from the cry it makes.

and when they choose to go from place to place, particularly in times of danger, they flatten out the body and slide off into space. The great width of the flattened body enables them to glide to the ground or to another limb, and in this way they escape.

The basiliscus lizards, eight to twelve
How do lizards move? inches long, live along the edges of swamps and rivers in Central America. When chased by an enemy, they

group of small lizards living in the warm countries the world over, have ridges across their toes which act somewhat like suction devices. This enables them to run across a smooth surface, and they are often seen running along the ceilings of houses in pursuit of insects.

The sea turtles are very ancient types of reptiles that have existed in somewhat their present form for more than 150 million years. Graceful swimming movements with flipper-like legs give them the appearance of flying through the water.

19

Are Reptiles Valuable?

These large marine reptiles stay in the ocean throughout most of their lives, coming ashore only to lay their eggs. In the evening, in early summer, many of the females come from the waters of the tropical Atlantic and Pacific to visit the sandy beaches along the coasts of the United States, Mexico, Central and South America. They make their way to a place above the high-tide mark, where they scoop out a shallow basin in the sand. In a period of two to three hours a turtle will lay from 100 to 150 eggs in this "nest." She then spends some time covering the clutch (a nest of eggs) by pushing and patting sand into it. No further care is given the eggs and they are left to the warm moist sand until they hatch. Turtles do not sit on their eggs as birds do.

Where do sea turtles lay their eggs?

The turtles (above) are laying eggs and covering them with sand for both warmth and protection. At the right is a snapping turtle hatching from its egg.

Fishermen along these beaches will seek out such nests, for the eggs are good to eat. The adult turtles are also sought as food. A prize catch is the large Atlantic green sea turtle, which weighs between 150 and 200 pounds. Its meat is tasty and it is also used for making turtle soup.

Can we eat the eggs of sea turtles?

Before the advent of plastics, the shells of hawksbill sea turtles, which measure from twenty to thirty inches, were extensively used for making fancy buttons and rims for eyeglasses.

In what ways are reptiles valuable to us?

In many shops we find leather goods made from the hides of alligators, snakes and lizards, including such items as purses, wallets, handbags, shoes, belts and many other articles. Not too long ago the Florida State Conservation Department had to pass a law forbidding people to take alligators from that state, lest they become extinct. Most of the leather now used to make these articles is imported from South America.

At Silver Springs, Florida and at San Butanton, Brazil, there are large snake farms where venom is extracted from poisonous snakes. This venom is processed and used as a medicine, which is very effective in treating certain kinds

part of their diet is made up of insects and rodents. It has been estimated that rodents destroy foodstuffs worth over 200 million dollars each year, so anything that preys on rats, mice, gophers and similar vermin is a good and valuable friend of man.

Reptiles of many kinds are found in the temperate and tropical countries of the world. They are of many different shapes, sizes and colors. One example is the thirty-foot giant gavial of Africa, a crocodile-like animal which lives along the Nile River and has an extremely long snout. Another is the wormlike blind snake, eight to twelve inches long, that lives beneath the ground in the southwestern United States and in Mexico. There are many forms that are only rarely seen, and others are commonly found near our homes.

How can we get to know more about reptiles?

of human sickness. Snake venom is also used to make the serum for the treatment of snake bite.

A small industry has been started in Florida for the canning of rattlesnake meat for food.

Perhaps the greatest service reptiles render to man arises from the fact that reptiles like to eat, and that the larger

A great deal of fun and education can be had by reading about the many kinds and by visiting zoos and museums where living specimens can be studied. However, the most interesting way to learn more about these animals is to go afield and collect them. The following lizards, turtles and snakes are not only interesting, but they are easily collected.

The lizard's tail, torn off by a bird, will regenerate (grow back to original form).

Turtles

PAINTED TURTLE

Spotted Turtle

The round orange-yellow spots on the black carapace (top shell) give the spotted turtle its name. These turtles, three to five inches long, are found throughout the eastern United States, where they live in the quiet waters of small ponds, lakes or swamps. Occasionally, they migrate from one pond to another and at these times they seek out the damp places on the woodland floor. Like many of the aquatic turtles, spotted turtles feed only when they are in the water. They use water to wet the food, thereby making a meal easier to swallow. Their food consists of worms, insects, fish and some aquatic plants.

How did the spotted turtle get its name?

The common spotted turtle makes a good house pet.

Specimens are found occasionally without spots and these can be identified by the smooth shell and the orange-yellow bands on the head. They make excellent pets, which soon become tame and feed from the hand.

Painted Turtle

This is one of the more common pond turtles that are often seen sunning themselves on a rock or floating log in the middle of a pond. When disturbed, they quickly slide into the water and bury themselves in the soft bottom mud or debris. They are easily identified by the mottled yellow to orange-red border of both the carapace and plastron (bottom shell). These markings and the stripes of yellow, red and black on the head are reasons for the name "painted turtle."

How did the painted turtle get its name?

They are found throughout the United States, except in the extreme west. They rarely leave the water where they catch their food—insects, salamanders, worms and fish. Young specimens are very attractive and are often sold by animal dealers and in pet shops.

BOX TURTLE

Box Turtles

Because of a broad hinge across the forward third of the plastron, box turtles can draw up their lower shell inside of the carapace. In this way they can completely "box" in all of the soft parts of their bodies as a protection against enemies.

How does a box turtle protect itself?

These turtles are favored as pets. They have a friendly disposition and can be freely handled. They are often seen roaming through woodlands and fields, particularly after a heavy rain, seeking insects, worms, berries and green vegetation. They are not aquatic, but they do not hesitate to enter the water and sometimes are found bathing.

There are four kinds in the United States, found from Texas to the Atlantic coast. All have yellow to yellow-orange stripes or markings on a carapace of deep rich brown. A specimen which had been in captivity for some five years became so tame, that whenever it was hungry, it would patiently wait near a feeding dish for its dinner.

Gopher Tortoise

The names tortoise, terrapin and turtle are really interchangeable. However, the word "tortoise" is generally used to name the kind that live in arid places, such as the Galapagos Islands off the coast of Ecuador. These islands are the home of the giant Galapagos tortoises that grow three feet in length. The names turtle and terrapin are usually used to describe those that live in or near the water.

Should we say "tortoise" or "terrapin" or "turtle"?

The gopher tortoises found in the United States live in sandy regions in many of the southern states between South Carolina and Texas. Unlike the other turtles, whose feet are flat and

The burrows of the gopher tortoise give it its name.

23

webbed and adapted for swimming, the tortoises have stumpy feet which are better suited for travel over the dry ground. The gopher tortoises make their homes in tunnels which they dig in the loose earth. At the far end of the tunnel, they excavate a small "room" in which they can turn about. In the wild they feed upon berries, grasses and insects. Specimens taken as pets can be fed berries, lettuce, apples and other fruit. In captivity, these reptiles like a pan of water in which they soak for long periods of time. Perhaps in the wild they get a great deal of moisture in their burrows.

The diamondback eats plants, worms and shellfish.

Diamondback Turtle

These turtles can be found along the Atlantic coast from Maine to Florida, and in the Gulf of Mexico from Florida to Texas. They live in salt and brackish water marshes and bays. At one time they were heavily hunted for food, but now their numbers are increasing. Small specimens are particularly attractive. However, collectors will find it difficult to keep them alive unless the turtles are provided with a tank of marine water with ample circulation. Adults can either be caught in the marshes or purchased at local fish markets.

The plastron is yellowish in color and **How did it get its name?** the large scales on the carapace have a series of whitish grooves, outlined against a gray-black color. The grooves, which are more or less diamond-shape in outline, are the reason for the name "diamondback." Many turtle farms where these specimens are raised are situated along the coast between Maryland and Florida.

Pacific Turtle

The good nature of the Pacific turtle **Can you feed it by hand?** makes it an excellent pet. It is very responsive when taken into captivity, and soon loses its fright. It will take food from the hand and, if regularly fed at a certain time, it will always be found waiting. It is a relative of the eastern spotted turtle, but is found only in the lakes, ponds and quiet streams along the Pacific Coast between Washington and California. Faint traces of yellow are found on the carapace, which has a ground color of soft olive-brown, and there is a mottling of yellow along

The Pacific turtle is about six to seven inches long.

the sides of the plastron. This reptile feeds upon crayfish, insects, some plants and fresh fish. A tank with a good supply of fresh water is needed to keep Pacific turtles happy.

Softshell Turtles

The sharp jaws and bad tempers of the adult softshell turtles, which are fifteen inches long, suggest that we avoid them. However, baby specimens are extremely interesting and are easy to keep. They feed upon crustaceans, fish, worms and insects. In captivity, they will readily take fish and pieces of meat. A well-fed specimen grows rapidly and, once tamed, usually remains friendly.

How do they protect themselves? In the wild, it often lies in the shallow water, partially buried in the soft mud. It occasionally extends its long neck and head toward the surface, and the tip of its long nose breaks through the water for air. This is a handy protection, because these aquatic reptiles with their soft shells, if discovered, would become easy prey to the animals that hunt them. When on land they can move with surprising speed, but they rarely stray far from water. If threatened, they will quickly dive down to the bottom where they hide in the mud.

A number of species in the United States are found in many waterways through the south and southwest and throughout the whole central region as far north as the Great Lakes. Occasionally, African softshell turtles are sold in pet shops in large cities. Large African specimens are as dangerous as the North American varieties, and should be handled carefully.

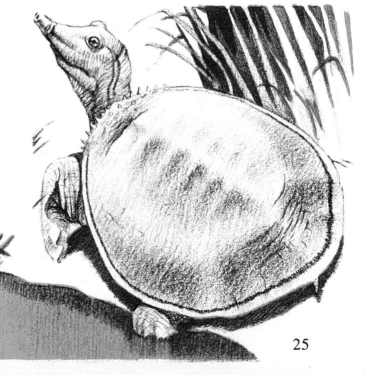

Softshell turtle

25

Lizards

It is easy to recognize the resemblance between the present-day lizards and the giant dinosaurs. Many millions of years ago, during the period when dinosaurs roamed the earth, there were many smaller reptiles clambering among the rocks at the feet of these giants. These smaller reptiles, which were the ancestors of our modern lizards, could easily hide from the "giants" and probably, in many instances, raided their nests and ate their eggs. It is possible that the smaller size of these early lizards, and their lesser need for food, helped them to survive, while the giant dinosaurs died out.

Why did the ancestors of the lizards survive?

Komodo Dragon

The largest of our modern lizards is the Komodo dragon, a ten-foot reptile which lives on the remote Komodo Islands in the Pacific Ocean. These lizards are so big that they can actually lift and carry away animals the size of a large dog. Many changes have taken place during the millions of years since the "age of reptiles," and the Komodo dragon may have descended from one of the much smaller prehistoric reptiles.

KOMODO DRAGON

The bearded lizard wears its "collar." When it is frightened, it extends the frills of skin around its neck.

Bearded Lizard

Most present-day lizards are small, and many have unusual shapes. One of the most impressive species is the frilled or bearded lizard of Australia. This lizard, eight to ten inches long, will raise the frills of skin around its neck into a very large collar when it is frightened. This makes the head appear to be three times its normal size and this undoubtedly scares its enemies.

How does it frighten its enemies?

Glass Snake

This long, slender, legless reptile looks like a snake. However, it has both eyelids and ear openings, which are never found in snakes. Glass snakes can be found in the

How does the glass snake trick enemies?

southeastern and central parts of the United States. Like many other lizards, they can break off their tails while being captured. This act is often a good defense, because the broken tail does not hurt the lizard and, as the tail lies wrig-

GLASS SNAKE

gling on the ground, it attracts the attention of the enemy. Meanwhile, the intact body of the lizard — minus the tail — crawls away to safety.

The snakelike appearance of these lizards and their extremely long tails are

27

probably responsible for the false stories about "disjointed snakes that will survive." In captivity, these lizards feed readily on insects, worms and small lizards. If care is taken when they are caught, the tail and body may remain in one piece. Broken tails cannot rejoin the body, but the glass snake will grow a new short tail.

their hind legs. The forelegs are folded under the body at this time. With a little imagination, we can picture from this pose what some of the giant reptiles must have looked like millions of years ago.

Collared lizards make their homes in rocky arid places in the southwestern United States. They feed mainly upon

The long-tailed, thin-necked collared lizards are numerous in rocky areas of the southwestern United States.

Collared Lizard

If taken into captivity, these lizards soon refuse food and die. It is far wiser to study this lizard, which is ten to fifteen inch long, in the field. Their name comes from the black or deep brown collar that girdles the neck. They are attractive but very nervous, and will usually bite if handled. If alarmed, they will race away on all four feet, lift the tail and forward part of the body off the ground, and run swiftly on

How does it get its name?

insects, but will also catch and eat small lizards.

Fence Lizards

The name "fence lizard" was given to these small spiny reptiles because they are often seen clambering over the stone and wooden fences that mark the boundaries of farms. Like most other small lizards, they will bite when first

Why do they bob their bodies up and down?

28

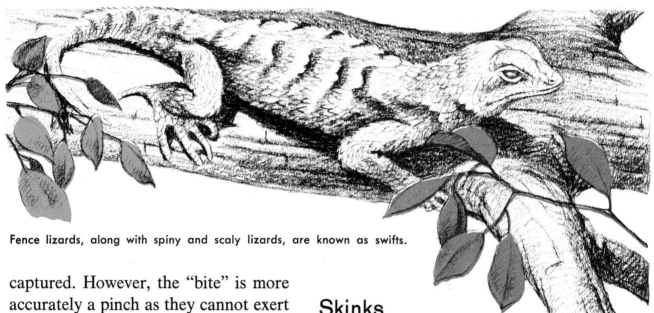
Fence lizards, along with spiny and scaly lizards, are known as swifts.

captured. However, the "bite" is more accurately a pinch as they cannot exert enough pressure to drive their small teeth into the skin. Soon after capture they tame down. The males are more brilliantly colored than the females and will sometimes bob their bodies up and down in a fashion that displays these bright colors. These movements are used both to frighten away other males and to attract a mate.

There are about thirty different kinds throughout the United States from the Atlantic to the Pacific, with the exception of the northern tier of states. They feed upon worms, insects and spiders. In captivity, their favorite food is the mealworm.

A five-lined skink of the eastern U. S. laying eggs.

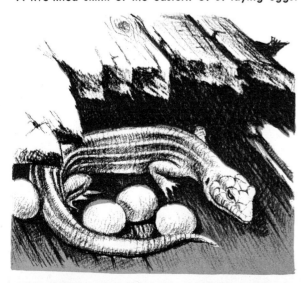

Skinks

Skinks are smooth waxy-looking lizards that usually live close to the ground. They have relatively short legs, long bodies and tails, and some kinds are very snake-like. The smaller species cannot hurt when they bite, but some of the larger kinds can inflict a painful pinch. It takes an alert hunter to catch them, because they quickly disappear either down the burrows they have dug or between the rocks and debris on the woodland floor. They are often found in moist, decaying logs.

They feed mainly upon insects, but larger specimens capture baby mice and birds. In captivity, they are long-lived if provided with plenty of moisture and a good hiding place. After they become tame, they may even take food — including mealworms and beetles — by hand.

Some species are brilliantly colored with stripes and have bright blue tails. The northern prairie skink, found in the north central states, has bright red cheek patches during the breeding season. Fifteen different kinds are found in the United States.

Horned Lizards

These curious lizards, sometimes called horned toads, are found in the middle and southwestern United States. Perhaps their flat, squat bodies, short stubby legs, and their sitting posture, caused the early naturalists to call them "horned toads." The presence of body scales immediately identifies them as reptiles. The long hornlike spines on head and body are probably a form of protection. However, hawks, owls, roadrunners, and other lizards are not deterred by these sharp spines when they feed upon the horned lizards.

Why are they called horned toads?

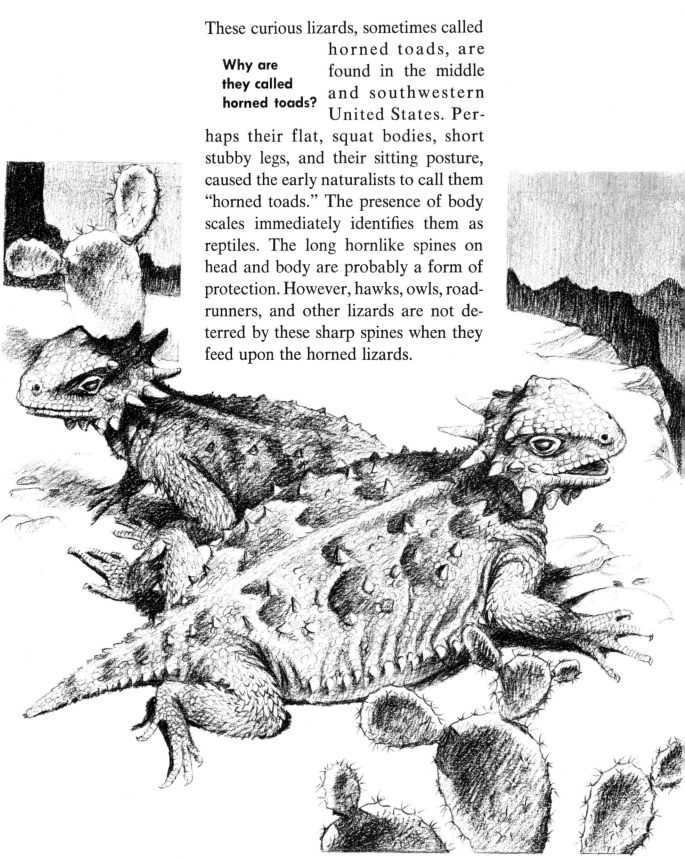

Horned lizards include such species as the short-horned lizard, desert horned lizard and Texas horned lizard.

The word *chameleon* comes from words meaning "ground lion." The American chameleon is also called an anole.

When danger threatens, these lizards will quickly bury themselves in loose sand or will puff up their bodies until they are almost twice their normal size. They also have the strange habit of squirting blood from the forward corners of the eyes, sometimes to a distance of several feet.

How do they protect themselves?

If kept at temperatures above 70 degrees Fahrenheit, they make good pets and will readily eat ants and other soft-bodied insects.

American Chameleon

This small, interesting lizard can change its body color. It reaches about six to seven inches in length and is found in the southeastern United States.

Under the lizard's skin are a number of tiny cells which are branched. They look like tiny trees. These cells contain a pigment (color). When the lizard is excited, frightened, suddenly cooled or heated, or moved into the light or dark, the pigments move to different places in the branches of the cells. If they move toward the surface of the skin, one color is dominant, or stands out. If they move away from the surface, another color is dominant. In this way, the lizard's color can change from dark brown to light green. During courtship and sometimes when the lizard is excited, it will extend a fold of bright red skin at its throat. The toes of this lizard, like those of the geckos, have adhesive-like tips which enable the toes to adhere to smooth surfaces. These small lizards make interesting pets, and readily feed upon mealworms and other small insects.

How do they change their color?

31

Snakes

The temperature of warm-blooded animals is always constant, because it is made by the animal's body. The snakes, as well as all other reptiles, are cold-blooded animals. The temperature of their bodies is controlled by the temperature of their surroundings. Those kinds that live in the temperate zones, where the winters are severe, find places beneath the ground or in the mud at the bottom of ponds, where the temperature never falls below freezing. Here they spend the winter in a deep "sleep" (hibernation). We do not find reptiles in the cold areas of the Arctic and the Antarctic.

Where do snakes spend the winter?

The reptiles that live in tropical countries, where the temperature is often very high, seek hiding places and wait (estivate) for the heat to pass.

Snakes are different from other reptiles in that they have no eyelids or ears. To hear, they sense the vibrations that are carried through the ground, and to protect their eyes they have transparent "caps" through which they see.

How do snakes hear?

When a snake needs to shed its outer layer of skin, it usually picks a quiet, protected spot. There it lies still for a few days while a special oily substance flows between the under layer of skin and the old outer skin, and then hardens. Then the snake moves about to find a rough log or stone upon which it rubs its head to loosen the skin at the edges of its lips. By catching the loose skin on a rough spot, it can crawl out of the old skin in about the same way that we might remove a pair of gloves from our hands — by simply turning them inside out.

How does a snake shed its skin?

This rattlesnake catches its loose skin on a cactus plant in order to shed.

King Snake

King snakes are found in most parts of
the United States. Their
What do they eat? name was probably derived from the fact that
they feed upon other snakes, even the
poisonous ones. They kill by constriction and are believed to be partially free
from the poisonous effects of venomous
reptiles. Besides eating other snakes,
they feed on rodents, lizards, insects and
birds, as well as the eggs of birds. They
live in many habitats, but the greater
majority seek the woodlands, finding
shelter in rotting stumps, under the loose
bark of fallen trees, and among rocks
and leaves.

They are easily managed in captivity
and can be handled
How do king snakes differ from coral snakes? freely. However, all
reptiles have individual
temperaments, so some
king snakes never tame
down. Collecting some of the brilliantly
colored king snakes should be done with

KING SNAKE

great care. Their coloring and pattern are quite similar to those of the very poisonous coral snakes. Coral snakes have a series of bright colored bands along the body and the colors red and yellow come into contact. These two colors never touch in the harmless king snakes.

Hognose Snake

How can you identify it? Its upturned snout is a good characteristic for quick identification when we find this short heavy-bodied snake in the field. The snout is used by the snake for digging. It will burrow beneath the surface of sandy soil in quest of toads, which are the main part of its diet. It also eats young mice and lizards.

When molested, this snake displays very unusual behavior. It **How does it "play dead"?** first flattens its head and spreads the forward part of its body, hisses loudly and strikes out at the danger with a closed mouth. If the annoyance persists, it will soon begin to writhe and twist its body as if in great agony. The hognose snake continues this behavior and finally rolls

over on its back, suddenly ceasing all motion. In this condition, it can be prodded without response. However, if we roll it over, right side up, it will immediately roll over onto its back again. Perhaps this snake believes that the only way to act like a dead snake is to lie upside down. They make interesting pets, and once these snakes feel perfectly safe, they will stop "playing dead." It is necessary to have toads available as a food supply for them.

Garter Snakes

Every state in the United States has its

Why do they give off a vile-smelling body fluid?

populations of garter snakes. These common snakes, which are eighteen to thirty inches in length, are known to every young boy who has spent any time in the field. They can be found in vacant lots, backyards and even city parks. They have a preference for moist places, because there they find their food which consists of worms, salamanders, fish and frogs. Young garter snakes will feed readily on insects. When these reptiles are first captured they will give off a vile-smelling fluid from glands at the base of the tail. The odor of this fluid probably repels their enemies. This habit stops as soon as they become tame.

Garter snakes are extremely easy to

How many young can a female garter snake have?

keep, because they can often be induced to take small pieces of meat and fish as a substitute diet. Care should be taken that large females are put into tight cages. A single female can give birth to as many as fifty or more

GARTER SNAKE

35

COPPERHEAD

TIMBER RATTLESNAKE

WESTERN DIAMONDBACK RATTLESNAKE

QUEEN SNAKE

WATER MOCCASIN

RAINBOW SNAKE

CORN SNAKE

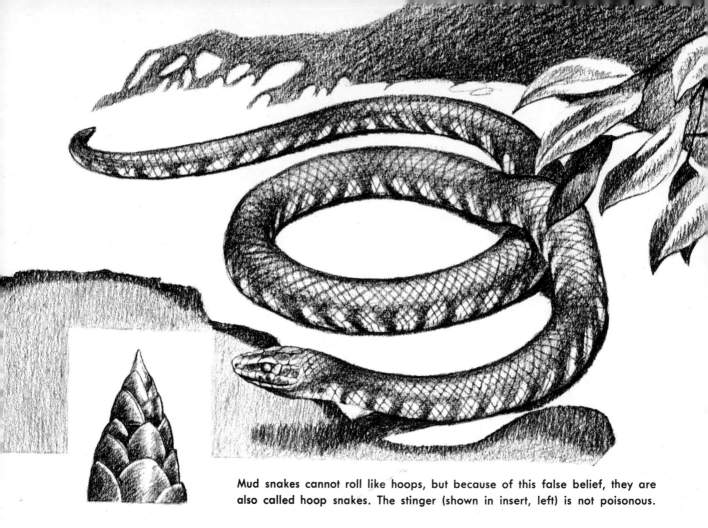

Mud snakes cannot roll like hoops, but because of this false belief, they are also called hoop snakes. The stinger (shown in insert, left) is not poisonous.

four-to-five-inch young. The name of this snake undoubtedly comes from its ribbon-like pattern, which is similar to that on the ribbon garters used by men.

Mud Snake

These long blue-black snakes are found in the southeastern part of the United States, and are four to six feet long. They are docile and can easily be tamed. They live along the fresh-water canals and swamps where they catch fish and large salamanders for food. The bright red patches of color on the sides and underparts of the body are in strong contrast to the black ground color.

However, the snake is not easily discovered, because it usually **Can it roll like a hoop?** hides in the muddy water when molested. The tail terminates in a sharp spine-like tip. When handled, this harmless tip will often scratch across the skin. This has caused many false stories to be told about the mud snake, such as: "It stings you with the end of its 'poisonous' tail"; "It can take its tail into its mouth and roll like a hoop." Both stories are not true, of course.

In captivity, these snakes should be provided with plenty of water. An aquarium tank, partially filled, makes an adequate cage. A large rock should be provided so that the snake can get up out of the water when necessary.

Small Snakes

Where can you find small snakes?

Twelve inches and under is the adult size of many snakes that live in the United States. The smaller varieties are as interesting and striking in appearance as many of the larger forms, and often they can be found close to human habitation. We can discover these reptiles by carefully turning over rocks, leaves and rotting wood that lie on the ground in a vacant lot, field or remote corner of the city park.

In the eastern and central United States we can find worm snakes, red-bellied snakes, De Kay snakes, ring-neck snakes, Florida brown snakes, rough and smooth earth snakes, and black swamp snakes. Many of these snakes are quite colorful. The red-bellied snake and the black swamp snake possess bright red ventral (underpart) scales. De Kay snakes have a soft brown dorsal

(upper) surface. When the animal is disturbed and puffs up its body, the dorsal surface turns into a checkerboard pattern. The ring-neck snake has a striking color and pattern. The undersides are either a bright red or orange red, the back is a glossy blue-gray, and about the neck there is a collar of bright yellow. There are also many small species in the western part of the United States.

All small snakes feed upon insects, worms, small salamanders and fish, and they can be easily tamed and kept for study in your own home "zoo."

Pictured above is a den of rattlers. Rattlesnakes are born alive and a litter of about one dozen is common.

How to Keep Reptiles

The most important thing in caring for wild animals is cleanliness. The cages have to be kept spotlessly clean and each animal needs plenty of fresh drinking water. Aquatic turtles and alligators can be kept in aquarium tanks which hold about one or two inches of water. A couple of large flat stones are needed, so that the animals can climb up out of the water. Clean these tanks at least twice a week and always be sure that the new water is the same temperature as that which was removed.

Feed the reptiles once a week by putting small pieces of raw fish or meat directly onto the stones. Any of the food not eaten has to be removed before the end of the day. Both alligators and turtles grasp the food and carry it off into the water before swallowing it.

Cages in which sand, earth, small cactus plants and other natural decorations are placed do look natural. However, it is difficult to keep this type of cage clean and it is not long before disease establishes itself. The best place to keep lizards, snakes and land turtles is in a small, simple, well-ventilated cage which is painted with a hard, glossy enamel paint. Such cages are easy to keep clean and dry.

The only foreign object that should be put into a reptile cage, besides a drinking dish, is something that will give the reptile a place to hide. An inverted cardboard shoe box, with a small hole cut in the side, makes a good reptile home.

The joy of learning about the living things around us can come from keeping a wild animal as a pet.

Reptiles make good pets.

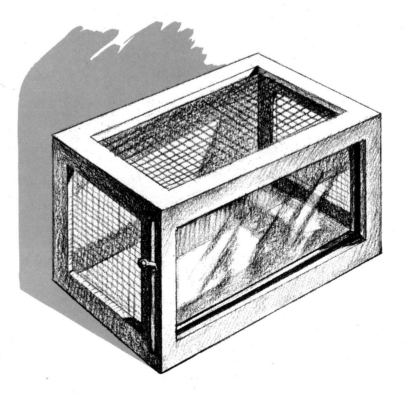

A simple, well-ventilated cage is the best home for your reptile.

CAGE FOR SNAKES

CAGE FOR SEMI-AQUATIC SPECIMENS

CAGE FOR LIZARDS

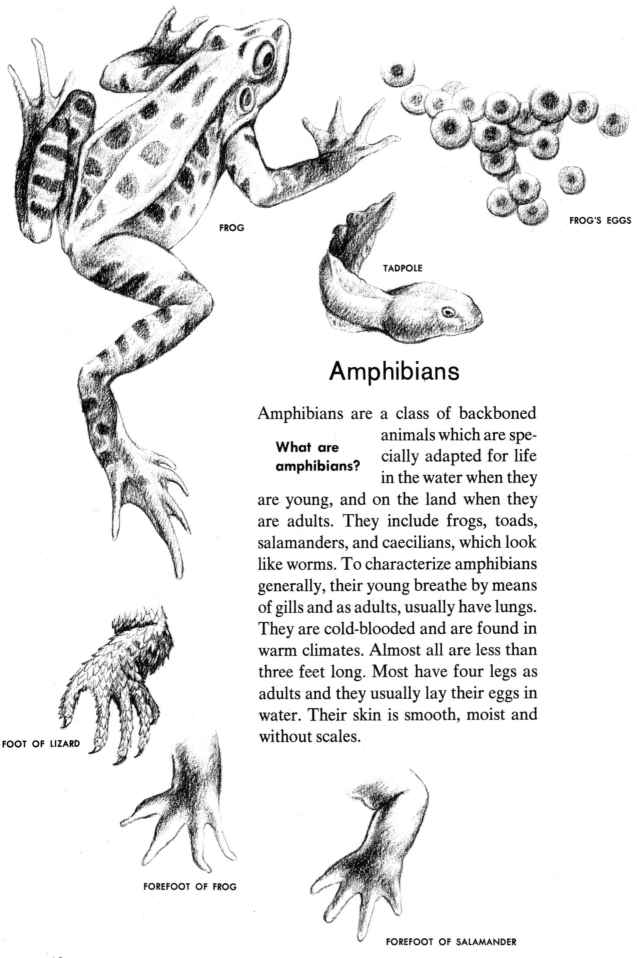

FROG

FROG'S EGGS

TADPOLE

Amphibians

What are amphibians? Amphibians are a class of backboned animals which are specially adapted for life in the water when they are young, and on the land when they are adults. They include frogs, toads, salamanders, and caecilians, which look like worms. To characterize amphibians generally, their young breathe by means of gills and as adults, usually have lungs. They are cold-blooded and are found in warm climates. Almost all are less than three feet long. Most have four legs as adults and they usually lay their eggs in water. Their skin is smooth, moist and without scales.

FOOT OF LIZARD

FOREFOOT OF FROG

FOREFOOT OF SALAMANDER

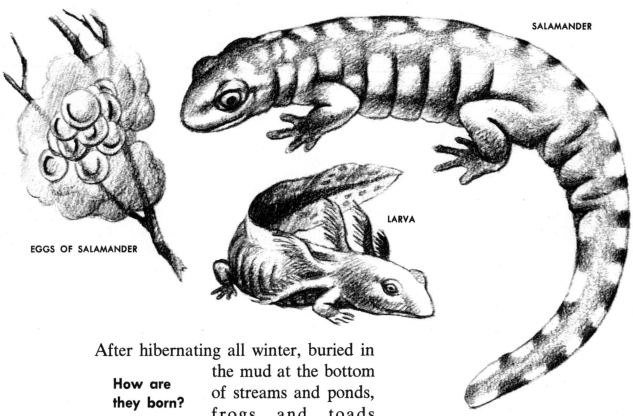

SALAMANDER

EGGS OF SALAMANDER

LARVA

SKIN OF FROG

SKIN OF LIZARD

How are they born?

After hibernating all winter, buried in the mud at the bottom of streams and ponds, frogs and toads emerge in the spring to renew their life cycle. The females lay eggs in a jelly-like mass, attaching them to twigs, grass, or stones in shallow water. In a short time — from a few days to a few weeks, depending on the kind of amphibian and the temperature of the water — the eggs hatch into tadpoles or larvae. These tiny creatures are completely on their own and soon learn to nibble at small water plants and hide from their enemies. Eventually, the tadpole's gills disappear, its tail shrinks, and it begins to grow legs.

TOAD CALLING

HOW TOAD CATCHES PREY

43

GREEN FROG

BULLFROG

BARKING FROG

GREEN TREE FROG

CRICKET FROG

RED-LEGGED FROG

NARROW-MOUTHED TOAD

AMERICAN TOAD

GREAT PLAINS TOAD

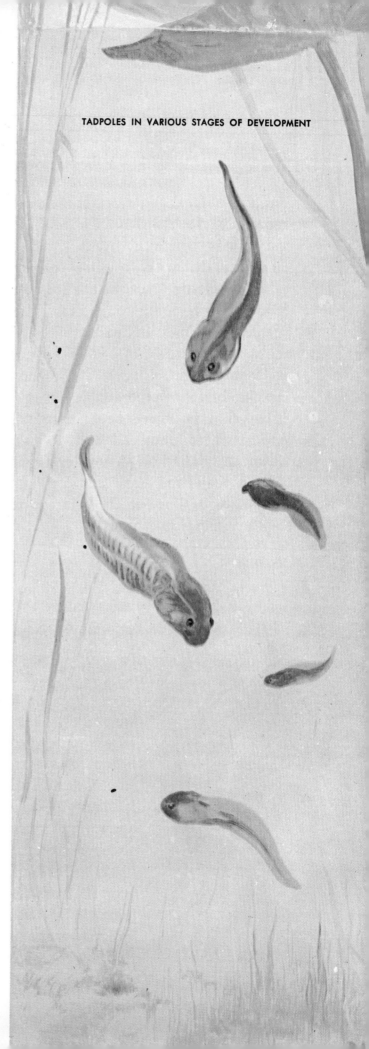

TADPOLES IN VARIOUS STAGES OF DEVELOPMENT

Wood Frog

What does it look like? Like many wild creatures, frogs are endowed with protective colors which blend with their natural habitat. For example, the wood frog is soft brown like the leaves and leaf mold in the woods where it lives. Looking closely at the wood frog, we can see other interesting characteristics. Its hind legs, long and strong, allow it to jump many times its own length, and the wood frog turns in mid-air to face its enemy when it lands. Its bulging eyes are bright-colored, like jewels, but it sees moving objects better than still ones. Its wide mouth allows it to gulp down its food whole — smaller frogs, worms, snails and small fish. Its long, sticky tongue flips out like lightning to capture insects in flight.

Wood frogs lay a mass of 2,000 to 3,000 eggs.

SPRING PEPPER

PINE TREE FROG

Tree Frogs

Can frogs climb trees? We usually think of frogs jumping on the ground, but tree frogs actually live in trees and shrubs, where they cling to branches with the help of sticky pads on their toes. These little frogs, no more than two inches in length, leave their airy homes only to lay their eggs at breeding time. There are several species in addition to the common tree frog, which has a dark patch on its back. The green tree frog is bright green and can change its color quickly. The Canyon tree frog has several round spots on its back, and the Pacific tree frog is striped.

46

Spadefoot Toad

It is difficult to distinguish between toads and frogs until we remember that toads have a rough or warty skin, that they are more plump and move more slowly than frogs, and that they do not always live near water. It is not true, of course, that toads will cause warts if you handle them, but when they are in danger their skin sometimes exudes a milky fluid. Most toads burrow into the ground, and the spadefoot toad is especially well

Do toads cause warts?

The spadefoot leaves its burrow at night to feed.

equipped for burrowing. It has webbed, spadelike feet which clear the way as it twists itself backward into the soil.

Newts

Of all the salamanders — and there are more than a hundred different kinds in the United States — the newt has the most interesting life cycle. Its eggs, similar to those of the frog, are deposited on leaves and stems of water plants. After hatching, the larvae live for three or four months in the water and then come out onto dry land. It is now bright orange in color with red spots circled in black on its back. After spending two or three years on land and growing to three or four inches in length, it returns to water for the rest of its life. The adults of the eastern newts then change color and develop a broad swimming tail which helps them move about.

What is the newt's life cycle?

Blind Salamanders

A great variety of salamanders is to be found in various parts of the United States. Among the aquatic species are the mud puppy, hellbender and Congo eel. Some salamanders have names descriptive of their color or markings: green, purple, red, painted, tiger, mottled and marbled.

Why is it called "blind"?

Salamanders are not as commonly seen as frogs and toads, because many of them come out only at night and all of them avoid the sun. One species, the blind salamander, usually lives in caves, and its eyes are either very small or undeveloped. Because it lives in darkness, its skin is pale yellow or white. These salamanders are found in the Ozarks, Georgia and Texas.

MUD PUPPY

SLIMY SALAMANDER

RED SALAMANDER

ALLIGATOR SALAMANDER

YELLOW SPOTTED SALAMANDER

PAINTED SALAMANDER

DEVELOPMENT OF NEWT

48

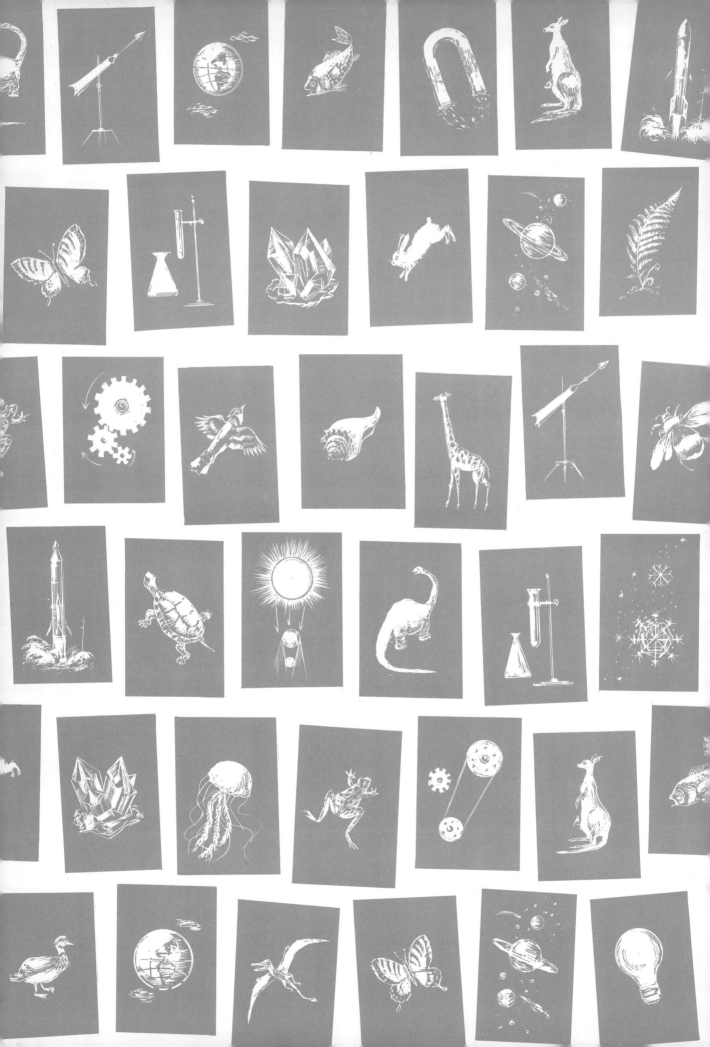